Falling Forward

How an Ordinary Kid Failed His Way to His Olympic Dream

JONATHAN HORTON

Published by

Scriptor
PUBLISHING GROUP

This book is dedicated to my parents.

Thank you for loving me and always making the sacrifices
that allowed me to live out my dream.

Table of Contents

How It All Got Started

I have been fortunate to experience a lot of amazing things in my life – I've travelled the world, met great people, and achieved athletic dreams most people will never have the opportunity to chase. However, there is a back story to it all that many people don't know. You've heard stories of the people who experience a lot of hardship but go on to do great things, right?

I am no different.

Sometimes, if you look back on things you did or the things that happened to you, it becomes obvious why it all unfolded the way it did. It isn't always obvious in the moment, but thankfully, my parents were intuitive enough to see the clues.

I was a rambunctious, crazy, and hyperactive child. I used to jump on the beds and climb the walls. I even taught myself how to flip on my parents' bed. Every time my parents would hit the button to the garage door, I would grab the bottom of the door and fly up to the ceiling as the garage door opened. I was an acrobatic monkey from day one.

In fact, my mom says I was basically flipping in the womb!

There was, however, one defining moment that started a ripple effect and plunged me head-first into my gymnastics career.

One day when I was four years old, my sister and I went shopping with Mom at a Target department store. I used to love grocery shopping and hanging out with Mom. We felt very lucky that she was able to be a stay-at-home parent. She actually had a very successful career in the business world before she had my sister, but sacrificed her job so that my sister and I could spend all of our time with her while Dad was at work.

On that day, she took us to the store like she always did. Now, I was that kid who occasionally had to wear the backpack with the leash on it because I was so wild. Unfortunately for Mom, there was no leash that day and she ended up losing me in the store. She was panicking; five minutes went by, then 10 minutes. Nobody could find me.

Mom is a four-foot-seven-inch little firecracker of a woman. She typically doesn't do really well in pressure situations, and from what she told me later, the entire store heard her freaking out. They all started searching for me, including the store manager.

Finally, the manager of the store spotted me, approached Mom, pointed to the ceiling, and said, "Ma'am, calm down. I found your son. He's way up there." He pointed to the top of a support beam in the center of the store; I had climbed about 25 feet all the way up. People were shocked and amazed that as a four-year-old child, I had managed to make the climb and hang out at the top. I was just bear hugging this big pole looking down thinking, "This is cool."

After I came down, we left the store, and Mom told Dad about the Target experience later that night. Dad said, "Wow. Our son, he's a freak. We should probably stick him in a sport like gymnastics." As a result, they enrolled me in classes at a gymnastics facility the very next day.

The rest of this book is going to show you how that decision became a defining moment in my life. My parents' choice allowed me, an ordinary, rambunctious kid, to go on to live an Olympic dream.

My First Gymnastics Experience

After that episode at Target, my parents realized I needed a constructive outlet for my endless energy. As you can probably imagine, gathering a bunch of four-year-old children for any reason results in organized chaos. You're herding cattle at that point – little kids are now running all over the gym, playing in the foam pits, and swinging on the rings and the high bars. Even though balance beam is not a boy's event, the instructors put young boys on a balance beam to help with coordination. Clearly, good balance is fundamental to success in gymnastics, so it made sense.

My two young children, David and Addison, have recently begun their own athletic journeys. As I reflect on those early moments in my life, I realize that their young minds are now being filled with many of the same amazing memories that I have. And yes, they are both wild and crazy just like their father!

For me, I loved gymnastics from the moment my feet entered the door. It was just a way for me to get some energy out, and that's what my parents wanted. That was their only goal with putting me in gymnastics, really. They realized that perhaps I had some type of untapped talent, but more than anything, I just had a ton of energy that needed to be released. So I went to the gym every few days.

I started out in a tiny recreational program in north Houston, and I took classes there until I was about six. I ended up showing a little bit of promise, so Mom and Dad started asking around for advice on a better training facility. Luckily, our next-door neighbors at the time had a son who was a very talented gymnast. They recommended that my parents move me to a gym called Jim Culhane's Gymnastics. The owner, who was obviously Jim Culhane, was a former gymnast who competed in the 1972 Olympic Games. Our neighbors warned my parents that Jim was a little unorthodox, but still one of the best in the business. I know Mom and Dad didn't totally understand what that meant at the time, but we were in for a wild ride with Culhane.

I remember being at Culhane's Gymnastics very clearly because Jim Culhane was militant. He had a crazy streak when he was younger, so he had seen and done it all. For example, he was once asked to leave a competition because he had hot-wired the head coach's car the night before. He also was known for streaking across the floor exercise at major international events, and even more surprisingly, skydiving in his birthday suit as well! However crazy he may have been, though, he had the pedigree and track record of an accomplished Olympian, so he was well qualified to coach six-year-old Jonathan. He was also a much different type of coach than I had ever had. Interestingly enough, I remember vividly getting yelled at as a kid – as a six-year-old – and I was so rambunctious that the guy could barely handle having me in the gym.

I know for a fact that I drove Jim insane. Honestly? I don't blame him. The truth is that not only was I rambunctious, but I also wasn't the flashy, super-talented kid who everybody thought was going to be a rock star. I was a slow learner back then, and I still am now. I think it's because I couldn't stay focused for very long. I wasn't the strongest or fastest kid in the gym, but there was something Jim Culhane saw in me. One day, after class at the gym, he surprised my family by moving me onto the competitive team.

My mom actually thought he was just trying to get more money out of us and told him, "There's no way he's supposed to be on a team yet. He's too young. He's not good enough."

Jim Culhane said, "Nope. I want to move him up to the team. I see something in him. There's something about him that we can work with. It's rare and not traditional, but there's something about him that just may work."

I have to give a lot of credit to Jim Culhane for seeing something deep down within me. He was so hard on me and on some of the other kids. He pushed us, but I think he might be one of the reasons my parents kept me in the sport. They eventually concluded: "Okay, this guy is a former Olympian. He owns this gym. He must know what he's talking about. I guess we'll go ahead and run with what he says. We'll stick Jonathan on the team." And just like that, I was on my first competitive gymnastics team.

I ended up staying there for a few years and saw slow improvement. I'm naturally a very competitive person and I always wanted to win, but there were tons of kids early on that seemed impossible to even get close to challenging. I can rattle off every single name of every single kid I ever thought was impossible to beat, starting with when I was six. I couldn't figure out how to be as good as they were. I couldn't learn the same routines. I couldn't learn the same skills. I wanted to be in the gym all day because I loved it there, but I just couldn't win anything. It drove me crazy. Every now and then I'd win a medal or a ribbon, but in the beginning, winning just didn't happen.

So how did my competitive career start? In the words of our current generation, "LOL!"

My First Competition

I competed for the very first time at the age of six, and my family still has it on video. First off, Jim Culhane, in his stern and militant style, had repeatedly told us what to do. My brain worked a little differently, though, and I'm pretty sure everything he said went in one ear and out the other. I was in la-la land the majority of the time as a kid. Regardless, my first routine was floor exercise. I walked up to the floor and stared at the judges as if I didn't know what to do. Jim Culhane reminded me to raise my arms up to let the judges know that I was ready. I did it, and then I stepped onto the floor and promptly forgot everything I was supposed to be performing.

I had been training there on the team for five, maybe six months. This was my first competition, and I had no clue what my routine was. Now, it's hilarious to go back and watch the old VHS recordings. I looked over at my coaches, and Jim is gesturing for me to do a forward roll, a cartwheel, a kick up to handstand, or whatever it was I needed to do. When I watch that video now, I see what Jim saw – a giant fire that simply needed to be lit and unleashed to burn brightly. I was this little mess of a kid on the floor who didn't know what he was doing, was super raw, and could barely do anything the way it's supposed to be done – but it was the energy that I think he saw. I had talent deep down, but it was going to take a lot of work to dig it up. Now I see it when I look at myself as a kid, and I see it in my own children.

I forgot my whole routine, but I stumbled through it. I went over to the vault for my next routine. I remember walking up to the vault and taking off before the judges were even looking. I also remember Jim Culhane loudly reminding me to go back and do it again when the judges were ready. The whole competition was a disaster, and that didn't really change for a few years. For me, gymnastics was just about the joy of being able to run, jump, and flip, and to have a blast throwing myself around.

There were many times that I came home from competitions and practices and would cry to my parents. I always called him Mister Jim. "Mister Jim was yelling at me, and he was so mean." One day when I was probably seven years old, I got a big blister on my hand for the very first time – we call them rips in gymnastics and they're very common. So I'd gotten my first huge rip on my hand, and I walked up to Mister Jim to show him my hand. He looked at me and he said, "Congratulations, boy," and he high-fived that blister! I definitely didn't appreciate it at the time, but now that I look back on it, I see that every single thing he did was to prepare me, discipline me, and teach me how to be tough.

Early on, I simply tried to wrap my mind around what I was doing. I was unlike so many of the other boys who seemed to be much more mature. They were able to listen and learn. I was the kid who was getting consistently kicked out of the gym for misbehaving.

In fact, I even got kicked out of a competition one time. Here's what happened:

My parents took me to a competition here in Houston. While I was at the meet, I saw a foam pit I wanted to jump in. My turn to compete hadn't come up yet, so of course, I was just goofing around. I was excited to be in a brand-new gym I hadn't been to before. Well, I jumped in the foam pit, and Mister Jim yelled from across the gym, "Get out of there! We're in the middle of a competition, and you're coming up soon!" I got out of the foam pit, and what do you know? Silly Jonathan Horton jumps back in the foam pit. He got on to me again. I got out, and of course, I had to do it a third time.

I'm telling you, I didn't learn anything fast, not even when someone was yelling at me.

Finally, Coach yanked me out of the foam pit and walked me up to my parents with a furious look on his face. Jim looked at Mom and Dad and tore up my scorecard, the paper the judges use to write down a gymnast's score after his routine, mid-competition. He said, "Take your son out of here." Now, my parents had paid a fee to get me into the event, and they were fuming because it was early on in the competition. They had probably paid $30-$50 for me to be there, and my entire family was there to see me compete, including my sister and my grandparents. Competitions for a six-year-old weren't exactly the most exciting things in the world, but they were still there to show their love and support. Unfortunately, none of that mattered because my coach had just sent me home.

Dad was mad and was about to get in Coach's face, but Jim said, "Bring it on." Now, Jim Culhane wasn't the biggest guy in the world, but he sure was an intimidating individual. He wasn't very tall (he was a gymnast, after all), but the guy was a little bit nuts. My father knew that, so he backed down. This wasn't the only time that my parents had issues with the way Coach dealt with me, though.

My parents didn't know much about gymnastics in those early days, and Jim's style was definitely a struggle for them.

In hindsight, we were all thankful for the way he treated me and the discipline he required of me. In a sport like gymnastics, a lack of discipline can lead to not only a lack of success, but also to potentially catastrophic injury.

When I was eight years old, I ran a Fun Run race in elementary school at 9 o'clock one morning. Gymnastics class wasn't until later that day. Dad always loved coaching me on different things, and he said, "Now son, don't take off and sprint from the very beginning, because if you try to keep the lead the entire time, you're going to wear yourself out. People are going to pass you up. Instead, stay close to the front and keep the leaders in sight."

I took his advice and purposely stayed in third place until I was 100 yards away from the end of the race, then I sprinted to the finish. I won the race! As an eight-year-old, I ran a sub-seven-minute mile. I have always loved to run, and I pushed myself hard to be fast.

Of course, I still went to my gymnastics class later that day. Before every day of training we had to run two laps outside in the parking lot, which was probably half a mile. The parking lot at Culhane's Gymnastics was big, and he timed our run because it was part of our warm-up. If a gymnast didn't meet the time, Jim made him do it again. Coach did this to set the standard. It was his expectation that we would be challenging ourselves from the moment we arrived at the gym.

I always made the time – except that day.

My legs were tired from pushing myself at the run that morning, and I didn't make the time. Coach said, "Okay, do the two laps again," so I did. Obviously, I was even more tired now, and I didn't make the time.

He said, "You can't go in the gym until you beat the time." My parents were standing there and told him, "Jim, he's exhausted. He ran this morning. You're making him run again." He responded by telling them, "If he can't make the time, he can't work out. He's not ready for gymnastics."

I was in tears because I was so tired and couldn't run anymore. The rest of the guys had gone into the gym and started their workout. I was outside in the parking lot by myself trying to run, and I couldn't beat the time. Dad got really frustrated and said, "We brought him all the way over here for gymnastics, not for running." We lived 30 minutes away from the gym, so driving there was a little bit of a commitment. Coach told us, "These are my rules. Take it or leave it."

We got in the car and we drove home.

Dad and Coach used to get into arguments regularly. They never actually turned physical, but it seemed to get pretty close. Now when I look back on the latter part of my career, I see that I was always one of the fastest and more powerful guys in the sport. In the years since training at Culhane's, Dad told Coach, "Hey, I just want to say thank you for pushing my son the way you did, for making him strong, for making him powerful. You knew things that we didn't know as parents."

I realize now that the development of our minds to come prepared to meet the standards Jim had set, no matter what else was going on in our lives, was crucial. It didn't matter to Jim that I ran a sub-seven-minute mile as an eight year-old-that morning. To him, that was separate from what we do in gymnastics. Looking back, I'm very thankful for that push.

Jim Culhane knew what he was doing. He created a base of strength, power, fitness, and speed in his athletes, and was able to produce some fantastic gymnasts. Because of this foundation, I stuck with the sport and had a lot of respect for him.

I wasn't the prodigy a lot of people think an Olympian must have been, but for whatever reason, Jim's belief in me kept growing. He continued to pursue me as an athlete and continued to pour his heart and soul into seeing me improve. I know he wanted to make me stronger, and he had a reason for every strategic move he made as a coach. Unfortunately, my time with Culhane wouldn't last long.

In 1995, when I was nine years old – just three years after starting with Mr. Jim – Culhane's Gymnastics shut down due to some personal issues he had. When his gym closed, I was devastated. I cried over it because I didn't want to leave. I had grown to respect the man who pushed me every day. I had a second instructor at Culhane's named Roumen Yordanov, also an Olympic gymnast, who was a phenomenal coach as well. I remember thinking, "I don't want to leave. This is where I want to do gymnastics. I have the best coaches."

Fortunately, the foundation that had been created was set. Jim Culhane's gymnastics gave me the tools I needed to take the next step… in a new gym.

A New Gym,
A New Start

After leaving Culhane's Gymnastics in 1995, I took my training to Cypress Academy of Gymnastics. I ended up training there for the rest of my non-collegiate gymnastics career. I was coached by Tom Meadows, who still, to this day, is one of my best friends.

Just to give you a little bit of a background, Cypress Academy started in 1983, and was not the big place it is now. It started out as a 5,000 square foot gym here in Cypress, Texas, where I currently reside. Today, Cypress Academy is an 80,000 square foot monster of a facility, and it's not the only location! There is another Cypress Academy about five miles away, and there's a third and fourth on the way. The owner, Aaron Basham, is simply phenomenal at understanding the business of the gymnastics world.

Aaron purchased the business from his father upon his retirement in the 90's, and has since continued to grow the Cypress Academy legacy. Back then, Aaron was coaching the boys' team as well. He, along with Bill Foster and Tom Meadows, was one of my first coaches at Cypress Academy.

Cypress Academy was a rival of Culhane's at the time. I didn't want to go to Cypress Academy as a kid, but it was really my only option because it was close to my house. My parents actually drove out of their way to take me to Culhane's because they believed in his system, but Cypress Academy was only five minutes down the road. It was pretty easy on my parents to make the transition. For me, on the other hand, not so much.

I wasn't good with change. I was introduced to the team and the coaches, and it wasn't love at first sight. I was not excited about having to train at a new place, and I was still really sour about needing to make the change in the first place.

I remember my first day like it was yesterday. I felt awkward being in a new gym with new coaches. Again, I went from Jim Culhane, who was militant, to Aaron, Bill, and Tom who all had their own unique styles of coaching. Aaron was more laid back as a coach and had a lot of wisdom not only in gymnastics, but also in business. The stern coaches, the guys that were really hard and disciplined, were Tom and Bill. Bill had produced Olympians before and was very intimidating to work with, and Tom was fresh out of a success-ful collegiate and elite career. He had big goals as a young, ambitious coach.

Tom was an NCAA national champion, and one of the best gymnasts in the country at one point. When he fin-ished school, he moved down to Houston. He and Aaron were roommates at the University of Oklahoma, and Aaron asked him, "Hey, why don't you come coach the boys here in Houston?" Tom got to Cypress Academy about a year before I did, and he and Bill were intense. I had gone from one hardcore coach to two of them! I soon realized, though, that my new coaches were some of the best. I had nothing to worry about.

If you talk to them now, I'm sure they'll say something like, "Oh, my gosh. When Jon came to us, he was bouncing off the walls. He was super raw. We had to fix so many prob-lems that he had." Jim Culhane, as good of a coach as he was, didn't have time to fix some of the issues I had as an athlete before he closed his gym. As a result, Tom, Aaron, and Bill had quite the project. I think they saw the same energy and spark within me, but they certainly weren't sure if it would ever amount to anything.

As it turned out, training at Cypress Academy was per-haps the best thing that could have happened to me at that point in my life. It was there that I connected with some amazing gymnasts who pushed me daily, and that's really what I needed.

One of those teammates was Chris Brooks, who was a year younger than me. For Chris and me, it was actually more of a reunion because we had met several years before. We went to elementary school together, but he went to Cypress Academy for his training while I was at Culhane's.

Chris became my best friend in the entire world very quickly. He was just like me - a crazy kid who was bouncing off the walls, had tons of energy, and was super hyperactive – but there was one major difference. Chris was one of the best 8-year-old gymnasts in the country. He was absolutely dominant. Finally, for the first time, I had somebody I could look up to. It didn't matter that he was younger than me! I wanted to be as good as him in every way. I wanted to win competitions, and he was the prodigy kid at Cypress that Bill, Tom, and Aaron loved to coach. He was so good, and I followed him around like a lost dog.

Chris was one of the reasons I started improving dramatically in the sport. One thing that made us not only good friends, but great partners was the fact that we hated to lose more than we loved to win. We were both extremely competitive, and we found ourselves battling each other every day. In the beginning, Chris beat me at everything. We made a competition out of anything we did together. Training with Chris really made a big difference in my life.

In fact, there are many people from my time at Cypress Academy who played important roles in my career. Another teammate who had a massive impact on me was Raj Bhavsar. He was five years older than me, and just so happened to be the best junior gymnast in the entire country. He was breaking records at the time, and everybody knew who Raj Bhavsar was. His gymnastics was power-packed, rapid fire, strong, and incredible. I did everything I could to copy Raj's way of training; he was my idol.

The success of the boys' program at Cypress Academy really came down to the committed coaches I mentioned before. Bill Foster was the head coach at Cypress for many years before Tom Meadows took over, and he laid the foundation for the careers of a lot of successful gymnasts. Bill wasn't even a gymnast himself! In fact, he was a football player in his youth. But while Bill was younger and still playing football, someone suggested that he should watch a little gymnastics. "We need some help with teaching the guys how to get stronger and faster," they'd said. Bill figured he could handle that, so he began coaching a small gymnastics team. The next thing you know, Bill had launched into a career that would continue for the majority of his life. Just prior to coming to Cypress, Bill coached the best of the best, like

1988 Olympian Lance Ringnald. He had spent a lot of his career at a very famous gym called Gold Cup in Albuquerque, New Mexico. Bill was a mentor for Tom and Aaron and really helped map out the plan for how to coach guys like Raj Bhavsar, Chris Brooks, and me. These were my peers, and we had a huge group of guys to train with and learn from. At Culhane's, I had a group of people to look up to, but it was different at Cypress. My team became my second family.

To give you an idea of how amazing the gym was, I'll need to explain a few quick things.

At the time, there were four levels of gymnastics for guys tracking toward elite status. First, there was the Future Stars level. As you might guess, this level recognized young up-and-coming talent, and Chris was one of the best Future Stars in the country. Next was the Junior level, and Raj was the best Junior in the country at the time. Then there was the Senior National Team, and finally the Olympic Team. Cypress Academy had athletes on the national team or tracking toward the national and Olympic teams at every level at all times.

So how did Cypress Academy have all of these incredible gymnasts for me to look up to and try to emulate? Without question, the success of this group was due to the level of expectation placed on us by Bill, Tom, and Aaron. I quickly realized that if I wanted to be good in this sport, I needed to do my best to hang with the "big guys" in the gym. This is when things really started turning around for me. Cypress was a game changer.

Times changed, though, and eventually Bill took off and opened his own gym. At this point, Tom Meadows took over the Cypress Academy Boys' team program as the head coach. Bill has since retired from elite coaching, and Tom has become arguably the best gymnastics coach in the United States of America. I say that as objectively as possible based on the number of successful athletes he has produced over the years. Mark Williams, the head coach of the University of Oklahoma's Men's Gymnastics Team, is absolutely in the running as well. Mark and Tom coach gymnasts during different phases of their development, so a head to head comparison is difficult.

To bring it all full circle, Mark was Tom's and Aaron's coach at OU and then became my coach when I went to Oklahoma later on. I was very lucky and blessed to have been coached by Jim Culhane, then to train at another gym that had the best coaches in the country, and those coaches were coached by another legendary coach…who later coached me. Did that make sense? Just know that I had the most ridiculous coaches anyone could have had. It's crazy!

You don't necessarily have to be blessed with all the talent in the world. If you can put yourself in the best situation possible, like I found myself in, amazing things can be done. As I continued to grow through the sport, it felt like I just kept being placed in front of great people. And I needed all the help I could get! I'm more grateful every single day that I had the opportunity to learn through mentors who taught me what it meant to work hard and focus on my goals.

I will always remember what those men taught me – that hard work can beat exceptional talent when the hard worker works harder.

Catching the Olympic Bug

I'm often asked about when I became interested in becoming an Olympian. I think a lot of people who make it to the Olympic level would tell you they were inspired by a specific athlete or perhaps a legendary sports team.

For me, it happened in 1996 when I was 10 years old and watching my first Olympic Games. The Olympics were being held in Atlanta, Georgia. Until this point in my life, I think I was participating blindly in my sport. I was just having fun, playing around, swinging on the ropes, and jumping in the pit, but when I watched those Olympic Games, everything shifted. It was the most pivotal, monumental, and game-changing moment for me because it was the first time I considered my goals for my career.

My parents and I were glued to the TV, and I'll never forget it. As a male gymnast, I obviously watched the men's gymnastics team. This was when some of my gymnastics heroes were elevated in my mind – guys like Blaine Wilson, three-time Olympian, and John Roethlisberger, another three-time Olympian. Those guys were all on the '96 team, and I witnessed Team USA's Jair Lynch win the silver medal on the parallel bars while the team placed fifth. I was blown away by what gymnasts at the highest level of the sport were able to do. Part of me was thinking, "I will never be able to do that!" While the other part of me was thinking, "This is so flipping cool (pun intended), man, the Olympics!" There's just something about the five rings, American flags hung all over an arena, and a huge crowd of people chanting, "USA, USA!"

That said, the greatest experience of that Olympics for me was actually watching the women's gymnastics team. Today, they're still known as the Magnificent Seven, but the drama that unfolded and gave them that title on the last night of the competition is forever etched in my brain. The most memorable part was watching the last two U.S. competitors.

Women's gymnastics is a little different than men's because instead of six events, they have four. After the first three events were completed, the last event for the USA was vault, and the last two gymnasts to compete were Dominique Moceanu and Kerri Strug. All they needed to do was hit their routines, and Team USA would have the gold in their hands.

They would each have two attempts at the vault, and Dominique Moceanu went first. She ran down the vault runway for both vaults, and didn't make it to her feet on either one. Needless to say, with a gold medal on the line, the world was shocked. No one could believe she had just fallen twice. The whole competition then came down to Kerri Strug's performance. She needed a heroic performance and to land at least one of her two vaults for Team USA to win gold. Kerri raised her arms to signal to the judges that she was ready, ran full speed down the runway and right toward an Olympic-sized catastrophe for Team USA. Kerri landed her first vault exactly the same as Dominique had moments before – with a fall on her landing. Everyone seemed to be holding their breath. The concern that Team USA was about to lose the gold medal, on arguably the most consistent event in the sport, was very real.

Kerri Strug's vault was tricky. It was called a Yurchenko 1½. For non-gymnasts, a Yurchenko is a backward-entry vault. These vaults require the gymnast to make sure hand placement on the vault is proper. After Kerri struck the vault with her hands, she would have to do two flips in the air with a one-and-a-half twist. She had landed it a million times, so everybody was shocked that she didn't land it and seal the deal the first time.

After Kerri's first attempt, Team USA still had a shot at gold because she was about to walk back to the beginning of the runway and make her final attempt. But there was a huge problem. When she stood up after her first vault, she was visibly in pain. She started limping her way back to the end of the vault runway to attempt her vault again, and the agony on her face was evident. She was grabbing her ankle, and everybody quickly realized she was injured badly.

Olympic commentator John Tesh said, "Oh no, Kerri Strug is hurt!"

The fate of the women's team was riding on Kerri Strug's shoulders, and I was on pins and needles at the edge of my seat. I had been cheering the women on with everything I had in me. In my young mind, I didn't totally understand what it meant to be an Olympic champion, but I knew it was a BIG deal.

Somehow, Kerri mustered up the courage and strength to run down the vault runway on an injured ankle (we found out later that she had two torn ligaments). In spite of the pain, she gave all of her effort and all of her might to do what she could for her team. Not only did she do the vault, but she landed it on one foot and stood up just long enough to receive credit for a completed vault.

The arena went berserk! As her coach scooped her up off the ground, I remember thinking, "Man, she has to be in so much pain." After the drama had finished unfolding, the team stood atop on the medal podium. The American flag was raised up into the air, and our national anthem started playing. There was so much pride in the room, and I remember thinking at that moment, as I sat frozen on my couch, "That's it. That's what I am going to go and do. I have no idea how I'm going to do it, but that's what I want. I'm going to compete at the Olympic Games. I'm going to win a medal for my country. I want to be last up, just like Kerri was for her team, and I want to put on the performance of my life."

In men's gymnastics, we use a proper rotation of competition called "Olympic order." The traditional event order is floor, pommel horse, rings, vault, parallel bars, and high bar. High bar is the last event and it's the most spectacular of them all. I couldn't stop envisioning the scenario in which I would be the last guy up on high bar with a gold medal on the line. The team would desperately need me to have the greatest performance of my life and if I did it, we would win. I just always had that thought, "I'm going to be the next Kerri Strug. I'm going to do this against all odds for team USA."

It's crazy, and I can't explain it, but from that moment on, with as little success as I had experienced, I absolutely knew 100% that someday that moment was going to come. There was just no doubt in my mind that it would happen. Throughout the rest of my career and everything I went through – all the ups and downs, the rollercoaster, the failures – I just always knew.

I had no doubt. I had a faith beyond anything I can even describe. Once I had my "why" - my reason for going into the gym day after day - and I had visualized my own spectacular moment on the Olympic medal podium, I *knew* the opportunity would present itself one day. I just had to keep moving forward.

As soon as I had this idea of Olympic glory in my brain, it was etched so deeply that I couldn't get it out. I knew I would be willing to do whatever it took in spite of how I started, the kind of athlete I was, and the level of talent I had. All it took was a moment of inspiration and the seed was planted for my own journey. It blew up into this massive, overly ambitious goal that people told me repeatedly would be too hard to achieve. But I just felt it had to be possible. One hundred percent, from that day forth, I was going to become an Olympian. There was no force on this planet that was going to stop me.

That said, it was in that moment that I noticed something that would become a lasting trend in my life. Once I declare something like that, I'm immediately tested.

My First Nationals

To be clear, the energy from that Olympic evening was tough to sustain. I would say it died within me over and over again, and I continually had to reignite the flame. With guys like Chris Brooks in the gym, and some of the other guys we trained and competed against, it often felt like it was impossible to win anything. There were days in the gym when I couldn't learn anything, I couldn't get stronger or I couldn't find the way to make a routine work properly. There were so many times when my brain was filled with doubts, but then I would think back to my why, what I wanted, and how badly I wanted it. Even in those moments when I was filled with doubt, my overall dream was still there. I still knew I was Olympic bound.

This was the time in my early days when I finally began to see big improvements. After my '96 Olympic experience, I qualified with Chris Brooks to a competition called Future Stars Nationals. It was a really cool competition where 50 boys were invited from around the country. There was a qualification process to get into this competition, so we went to a little regional qualifier, and then we went to a bigger qualifier, and then in the end we were invited to go as two of the top 50 boys in the country to Future Stars Nationals.

The top 15 of those 50 boys at Future Stars Nationals would make the Future Stars National team, and that was the ultimate goal. If you made the National Team as a kid, the National Team coaches would recognize you as one of the up-and-coming hot shots. Those top 15 kids would be the ones they would start preparing to become Olympians in the future.

Chris and I were super pumped to go to this competition together. We were both thinking we were going to do very well and make the top 15. For me, it was the first moment I thought, "All right, I'm finally going to shine big and show people that I'm capable of greatness. I'm going to show everyone I can do this and that I'm a good gymnast. I know I haven't had tons of success yet, but I can be one of the best." I wanted so badly to be one of those guys that explodes onto the scene and proves himself in a big way.

We got there and started out the competition really well. Chris and I started on rings, and we both did awesome routines. In fact, we were both doing very well through the first five events. Everything was going according to plan; I would even say that we had caught fire! Finally, we got to the very last event - the pommel horse. From day one, pommel horse had been my nemesis. In fact, it was always my worst event. It's an event that's traditionally better for longer, leaner gymnasts. I was short, compact, and muscular, and I could never really figure it out. Toward the end of my career, I was able to survive it, but as a kid I fell all the time. I've got videos of myself falling off the event six or seven times in one routine – people were laughing! Okay, maybe they weren't random people. Maybe it was just my parents who were doing the filming (we all laugh together now).

At Future Stars, I'd had such a good day. Chris and I were both in the top 15 going into the final event. I think Chris was even sitting in first or second at this point. He went up to the pommel horse and nailed his routine, just like we all knew he would. My coach looked at me and said, "Hey man, don't do anything special here. You've done this routine a thousand times and you don't need to try to be perfect. Just get through the routine and we might be able to accomplish this goal today."

My turn came up, and I walked up to the horse. I remember being super nervous because it was my worst event and my most inconsistent routine. I told myself, "Come on. Just get through this." I raised my hands for the judges, jumped up to the horse, and immediately my hand slipped off. I did a 360° spin on my back on the horse, and I landed, flat on the ground. Stunned, I stood back up because I had to restart my routine. I placed my hands back on the pommel horse, jumped up, and proceeded to do the exact same thing.

I ended up falling six times on my pommel horse routine that day, and I scored a 1.9. On a scale of 1-10, a 1.9 isn't exactly helpful!

At the end of the competition, I ended up being ranked number 50 out of 50.

I was in dead last.

I was absolutely devastated. I was so upset, especially because my teammate had made the national team and I wanted more than anything to be there with him. Being dead last was not only unacceptable, but it completely crushed my spirit.

The emotions poured out of me. When I was young, I was the kid who cried when I failed or did poorly. I cried a ton, and I wondered if I was ever going to catch my break in this sport.

I remember being so hurt and jealous, because Chris got to go to the Olympic training center every few months for training camps as a member of the National team. He trained with the best guys, with the best coaches, and at the best facilities. Meanwhile, I was just hustling and grinding away back home, while the kids on the National Team were taking their skills to the next level.

As frustrated and upset as I was, I realized that I was also angry. It made me realize how badly I wanted to find success in this sport. Now I wanted it more than ever. Future Stars Nationals taught me a valuable lesson that I carried forward from then on. In that moment when I felt like quitting, I made the decision to do the complete opposite and not take the easy way out. Not only did I *not* quit, but I decided that I was going to do 100 times more. A lot of people in the business world talk about 10x-ing. As I look back, I think of every single time I failed, and how I 100x-ed. I just put the gas pedal to the floor and worked even harder. I told myself, "I'm going to do more. I'm going to do more. I'm going to do more. I'm just going to inch closer. I'm going to get a little bit better every single day."

It's funny how life plays out sometimes. My experience at the Future Stars competition is one of the moments that I look back on and laugh about. Gymnastics is not typically a sport of longevity. It's about who can last, who can put up with the garbage, who can put up with the failure, the hard times, the heartaches, the hard work, the pain, and the injuries. At the end of the day, I had committed to putting up with those things. So, out of all 50 of those guys at that competition, I was the only one who went on to become a two-time Olympian with two Olympic medals. From the bottom to the top!

I started out so poorly, but it was my mindset that was the key. It was the vision. It was the desire from every single one of those moments that pushed me forward.

Chris and I continued to train together, and as much as we loved hanging out as friends, we never lost sight of our dreams. We continued to press on. We told each other, "Man, one of these days we're going to go to the Olympics together, and we're going to tie. We're going to tie for the Olympic all-around gold, and our team is going to win gold, and we're going to do everything together." At the end of the day, we never made an Olympic team together. But Chris Brooks made the 2016 Olympic Games and was the Olympic Team Captain. Our dreams came true, just not at the same time.

Chris and I started gymnastics with a lot of other gymnasts who had big dreams and ambitions, but out of all of the guys who began that journey with us, Chris and I finished. In spite of the obstacles we faced, we refused to quit. We had each other's backs too. I never let him quit, he never let me quit, and we finished what we started. There was just something special about that brotherhood, about the connection between the two of us. We didn't accomplish everything we had imagined because we'd set some pretty lofty goals, but we did what we said we were going to do. We knew what we wanted, we never quit, and we became Olympians.

For me, it had all started as a kid in last place at a Future Stars Nationals Competition.

Redemption

I went back to the Future Stars competition the next year. Future Stars was open to 10, 11, and 12-year-old kids, and I ended up finishing in second place in the 12-year-old division. Needless to say, it felt pretty good to jump from 50th to 2nd in one year.

After that, I continued to train (and train and train), and I remember constantly placing second, third, fourth, or fifth. I would get really, really close to winning meets, but I always came up short. I started competing at the Junior Olympic Nationals when I was 14 years old. My very first one was in 1999 when it was held in Houston, Texas, and I did the same thing I always did – melted down. It's almost like any time I ever stepped up to the next level of the sport, I bombed. Worst. Competition. Ever.

The same thing happened at Junior Olympic Nationals as it did at my first Future Stars meet. Chris made the Junior National team, and I bombed horribly and didn't even get close. But the next year, we came back, and we both made the National team – just like what happened at Future Stars our second time through.

This is when I started getting better.

In fact, I won my first meet when I was 15 years old. It wasn't a huge event like Nationals, but I do remember where it was because it was such a big moment for me. It was at a competition called the Peachtree Classic in Atlanta, Georgia. I won the meet and I remember thinking, "How in the world did I do that?" I don't even remember how the competition went, but I recall being shocked by my placement at the end of the day. While I was standing on top of the podium, I thought, "What just happened? Did everyone else blow it? There must not be anyone good at this competition. The scores must be wrong!"

The breakthrough had begun and the giant weight on my shoulders had been lifted. After I had my first taste of that first place podium, I won another competition. Then another one, then some more. I was on fire! Then, as a junior in high school, I made my first giant leap into the big leagues when I became a national champion.

When I was a teenager, we called nationals at this level "JO Nationals" for "Junior Olympic," and I was officially the JO national champion. It was during this period of time, when I advanced to the highest junior level before I gained "Elite" status, that I started competing against some guys who would become a very important part of my future.

Let me introduce them to you.

There were a few guys that seemed to win everything at that time. Chris continued to be a rock-solid competitor, and there was another named Sho Nakamori who seemed unbeatable. He was winning JO Nationals in the division above me before he and another guy named Alexander Artemev began battling back and forth with each other. Those two were so far ahead of their time and the rest of the competitive field that it seemed easy for them to dominate every aspect of the sport. When I moved up to that next level, I was always way behind them. Once again, I felt I could never rise to the ability of the people around me.

There were a couple of other gymnasts at the more advanced levels who seemed nearly impossible to keep up with. One of them was Joseph Weaver, and another, named Taqiy Abdullah, was one of the most talented gymnasts I have ever known. Toward the end of my high school career, Taqiy Abdullah was the guy I personally battled for title after title. He was crazy good and from the first time we ever competed together, I thought, "No way! That kid is doing Olympic level stuff and I'll never be that good." Let's just say he won a bunch. But in typical Jonathan Horton fashion, after a long time and a lot of doubts along the way, I was able to beat him as a junior in High School. I became the Junior National Champion in the upper division. Of course he reclaimed that title our senior year, but still! We played a game of back and forth for many years to follow, and it drove both of us crazy.

What was really cool about all of this was that Taqiy, Joseph and I all ended up going to the University of Oklahoma together. A year after that, Chris Brooks joined us. We were all teammates, and we were like the Avengers of the college gymnastics world. It was as if we could combine all of our powers to become Captain Planet … I know I'm aging myself with that reference.

Bottom line? We felt like an unstoppable collegiate force and loved every minute of it.

Oklahoma!

Competing in college was fun and challenging. Having guys on the team I had known for years, who came up through the gymnastics ranks with me, was a fantastic experience. We expected to dominate, and we did. OU is a respected national powerhouse in gymnastics, so the decision to compete there made a lot of sense.

We won the National Title my freshman and sophomore years. During my junior year, we narrowly lost the title to Penn State. It surprised us because we didn't think we were going to lose, and to this day I'm not sure it should have been that close. That being said, I have tremendous respect for their head coach, Randy Jepson, and I am still close to some of the guys that were on that team. But we were disappointed with the result... maybe even a little bitter.

That outcome fueled the fire during my senior year. That year, we beat Stanford for the national title and regained our status as the best team in the country. We really came together, and we experienced a lot of special moments as we reminisced about the times we competed against one other throughout high school, battling back and forth only to end up one day being on a team together. Every collegiate moment with those men was magical.

When we were kids, we were in it for ourselves. Individually, we wanted to win everything and that rivalry reigned. But in college we realized, "Hey, we're in this together. Imagine how good we can be by training as a team!" Our one goal was to be NCAA team champions, because in collegiate gymnastics, that title is more important than the individual all-around or event medals. Every single team and every athlete has one dream in college, and that's to hoist up the golden NCAA team trophy. Becoming an NCAA national champion, as a team, was everything.

That team mentality took a short bit to evolve, though.

If I'm completely honest, I started my college days with a pretty horrible attitude. When I went to college, people always asked me, "Hey, what's your goal going into the NCAA scene?"

I said, "I'm going to be a four-time all-around NCAA champion." I had become this cocky kid who had won nationals a few times, and I just wanted to keep winning for myself. The thought of helping my team was completely absent from my mind. I remember when I arrived at Oklahoma with my freshman teammates, Taqiy Abdullah, Joseph Weaver, and Jake Messina. We had seven or eight seniors at the time who quickly put us in our place regarding the order of our priorities. It was all fun and games, but I quickly realized that this was no longer about me. This was about my team. These guys quickly became my family; they'd become my brothers.

Once I figured out how to compete for the guys who were standing by me and not for myself, my ability as a gymnast shot through the roof. I learned how to compete unselfishly and it gave me a new kind of power. Now when I was raising my hands to go on the floor, the pommel horse, the high bar, or whatever event I was on, I would think, "I have to be the best I've ever been for those men I train with. Those guys are depending on me to do my job. I don't want to let them down."

That was the beauty of collegiate sports for me. That's when I became a team player. That's when I developed my ability to lead, not just by what I said, but by how I trained and how I pushed other people to their best. I have to give all of those guys, all my teammates, all of my coaches, and the University of Oklahoma so much credit. They helped me evolve out of being an arrogant kid and into a leader; a team player that the others trusted to go into battle with. I look back now and can't help but think about what a phenomenal transition period that was for my life.

The shift in my mindset continued to help me improve dramatically year by year. I was aware of the fact that I was being tauted as a rock star on the team, and I did my best to be humble in that role. By my second year at Oklahoma, I was one of the best gymnasts in the country. My freshman year, when I was competing against guys who were much older and more experienced than I was, I got third place in the all-around. My sophomore year, I claimed the individual title. Taqiy won our junior year (of course!), and then our senior year, I took second again behind a gymnast named Casey Sandy from Penn State. I finished in the top three all four years during college, but none of my individual accomplishments mattered that much to me. I was proudest to leave college with the ability to say that my team had won three of the four years I attended school.

That period in my life taught me so much about the value of doing things for other people more than for myself. Yes, I went to college to earn a degree, but I believe that the most valuable information I received during my four years of school was how to set my own pride and goals aside to be a part of something greater – a team.

Temptations and Self-Discipline

Of course, the journey to becoming the best gymnast I could be had challenges, especially in college. Going to school was a huge adjustment for me, as it is for any college freshman. I freely admit that I was a mama's boy growing up. Mom did everything for me. She cooked my food, did my laundry, and really took care of me well. My mom is one of the three greatest women on the entire planet (I'm now a married man with a daughter, after all)!

But when I went to school, I had to learn how to do all those things for myself. I didn't know how to cook, so I was eating Chef Boyardee, Ramen noodles, and pizza rolls for the majority of my college career. I'm not proud of it! I really wish I had known then what I know now about nutrition, proper sleep habits, and overall wellness. Fortunately, I did learn.

I made some changes, but it was tough and a slow process. There were a lot of temptations to be part of things in college that I knew were detrimental to my training and my overall goals— things like going out, partying, and drinking to excess like I had witnessed so many other people do. I was able to stay away from all that stuff... for a while. I'm proud to say that I didn't drink my first beer until my 21ˢᵗ birthday. Even some of the guys on my team would say, "Hey, Jon. Why don't you come out with us, man? Have a good time! You've got to cut loose sometimes." I was just laser focused on my goals, and I knew what I wanted. Honestly, I didn't care if others thought I was lame or not.

I certainly didn't want to seem pretentious or judgmental with regard to my "good behavior" back then, and I want to be careful about it even now. But I do believe that my choice to abstain from a wild party life in school gave me a competitive edge.

When you have a highly-focused goal, you know what you need to do – and often what you need to avoid – in order to achieve it. Even my non-gymnastics friends would say, "Why don't you go have a good time? Quit taking this gymnastics thing so seriously."

But for me, it was serious. I was in college to get an education, but I never forgot about my ultimate goal. I wanted to become an Olympic champion. I think a lot of my teammates understood and respected that, but still they wanted me to have a good time. I can't blame them for looking out for me and trying to get me to relax from time to time.

Sometimes I wonder if I should've experienced college a little differently, but ultimately I'm thankful for the way I did it. I don't know if I would have become the athlete that I did if my choices had been different. I still believe that I wasn't the most talented athlete. I just worked my way to where I was, and I continued to need all of the help I could get. It was a struggle for me at first not knowing how to transition to being on my own, how to eat and sleep right, and take care of myself in general. But as I figured it all out and learned to stay away from the temptations, I learned how to truly commit to my goals as an athlete. My "why" was big, and learning to adapt in a way that was conducive to success was very important.

For the most part, I don't think people mean to pull you away from your goals or try to tempt you – if they're truly your friends, they just want to see you have fun. I always thought to myself, "Man, people just don't realize how badly I want this. They just don't realize how important this stuff is to me." It was so important to me that I was willing to make those sacrifices, and I always assumed I would stay connected to these people and have fun some other time... once the mission was completed.

I'm thankful for that mindset, but it was a challenge. During a few points in my journey, I almost gave in.

In school, we had morning training sessions that I HATED. Nonetheless, I woke up at 5:00 AM every day, went to the gym at 6:00, and went to class after that. I should note here that I wasn't the best student in the world. As a young kid, I received As and Bs, but it was because I gave school everything I had. I was always frustrated with those kids who seemed to do the bare minimum and continued to breeze through every class with an A. I just had the hardest time staying focused. My mind was always in la-la land, daydreaming about something ridiculous like battling dragons and flying like Superman. The only classes I was ever good at were math and science, and that's because I found them interesting. In every other subject, I was pretty pitiful. However, I really committed to getting better grades when I was in high school. There, for the first time in my life, I was able to earn straight A's a few times.

I honestly don't think it was an issue of intelligence. I just had no ability to focus. As I got older, I was able to learn to focus and I poured all of it into training.

Classes in college were incredibly hard, though. To this day I have a hard time sitting still for any length of time - writing this book has been a challenge! In fact, my wife tells me several times a day to stop bouncing my legs or tapping my hands. I just have to keep moving.

My inability to settle down hurt my test-taking ability too. I didn't do well on my SAT exam – I believe I got 1000 out of 1600. Imagine a hyperactive kid like me trying to sit through a five-hour exam. That did not work well! I even got bored and decided not to take a whole section of the reading portion. I remember thinking, "This sucks, I'm done." So I got up and left the exam. (Students- I do not recommend or endorse this decision).

Luckily, I got into Oklahoma and continued to thrive in the math and sciences classes I loved. I took Calculus III simply because I enjoyed it, and for no apparent reason, I'm freakishly good at it. I think I scored a 95 in that class. I also received a 100 in Astronomy, and I did really well in physics and chemistry. Courses like English or anything related to writing were a completely different story – the idea that I'm currently writing my second book still boggles my mind. There was also one class that I got a D in and I had to retake. Believe it or not, it was accounting. You would think that being good at math meant being good at accounting, but I was bored to tears and I couldn't figure it out. I'm still not convinced that I earned the "C" grade I received the second time I took the class. I'll never forget the day I took the final exam for that accounting course. I studied day after day and I thought I was totally prepared. For the first time in my entire life, I remember leaving the exam thinking, "Man. I can't guarantee that I got even one answer correct." It was even multiple choice. I think the professor just felt bad for me, thought I was hopeless, and passed me. Hey, a win is a win!

My entire schedule in college was a challenge. I was trying to balance my education and my gymnastics career, and it proved to be difficult at times. I would finish my morning workout, take a shower, drive straight to my first class, go to classes for four or five hours, drive right back to the gym for three or four hours, and then from the gym I would go to evening business classes. Those evening classes would end around 8:00 or 9:00 p.m. After that, I'd go home and try to study a little bit before going to sleep.

Then, I'd do it all again the next day.

Those were some of the hardest times in my career, but I learned so much about my character during that season of life. I feel like I built up my endurance as a human being during that time, too. I was committed to finishing college and becoming an Olympian; it was difficult and exhausting, though, and there were many days that I wanted to throw in the towel.

I'm thankful I didn't, and I'm forever grateful for what I learned from those challenges.

Love Connection

During my freshman year at Oklahoma, my life changed forever. While I was sitting in the cafeteria at lunch, a beautiful young lady named Haley Deprospero walked into the building, and captured my attention like no one ever had before. My eyes lit up, I sat up a little taller (or as tall as my massive 5'1" frame would allow), and I couldn't stop looking over at her. I tried to be discreet, but I'm pretty sure my obvious staring made it impossible.

I learned that Haley was a gymnast and was visiting Oklahoma on a recruiting trip. One quick note for those of you that are unfamiliar with how athletic recruiting works in the NCAA. Colleges will often bring recruits in to check out the schools they are most interested in attending. For example, I was recruited by Ohio State University, Iowa, Penn State, Michigan, and of course, Oklahoma. As a recruit, I went on recruiting trips when I was a senior in high school. Universities will fly potential athletes out to the campus, explain how or why the school is best for that particular athlete, and show them around.

Haley was being recruited heavily by several schools as well, but her interests were in Stanford and Oklahoma. To get into Stanford, you have to be brilliant, which she was. She had top scores in all of her high school courses and exams. In fact, she earned some of the highest scores possible on the SAT and ACT, and before visiting any schools, she had already been given several full scholarship offers. She was a top-notch student and a standout athlete, so it made sense that Stanford and the University of Oklahoma really wanted her. Fortunately for me, her mom, dad, uncle, and sister had all gone to Oklahoma. If it weren't for that long line of Oklahoma grads in her family, I'm not sure she would have ever visited. I'm glad she did.

Interestingly enough, she arrived on the Oklahoma campus dead set on attending Stanford and becoming a physician. She had already visited the Stanford campus and loved it. Then again, how do you not love Palo Alto, California? It's amazing. She was determined to go there.

However, on the day I laid my eyes on her, I started praying that she would choose OU. Haley and her family walked in, and I remember looking over at my teammate, Jake

Messina, and saying, "Dude, that's my girl right there." He just started laughing. I was like, "Man, I haven't even talked to her yet, but there's something about her. That is my girl."

I have never had a natural ability to talk to women, but I gave it my best shot while she was there. All the recruits and the men's and women's gymnastics teams ended up going out to a restaurant one of the nights while she was visiting. After 10:00 p.m. the restaurant turned into an 18-and-over dance club, and that was my chance to get to know her a little. I had a pretty grand plan of sweeping her off her feet that night. Let's just say I failed pretty epically on my first shot. It was no different than my gymnastics career. I was used to it!

I did everything I possibly could have done to talk to her and she wanted nothing to do with me. Eventually, she told me her name. Win? I tried to dance with her and talk to her throughout the night. I even tried to tell really lame jokes! At one point in the night, after trying my best and refusing to be defeated, I told my teammates, "Guys, I think that girl is going to kiss me by the end of the night."

They told me, "Dude, you do not have that kind of game."

I told them, "Just watch."

She must've thought I was the dumbest person on the entire planet… and my hindsight tells me she might have been right at the time. At the end of the night, I had officially failed miserably in my pursuit. We were in the parking lot, and I went up to her, and I said, "Give me a break here. Can I at least get your phone number?"

She gave it to me, and I actually called her a couple days later. She had already gone back to her home in McKinney, Texas.

The conversation went a little bit like this. I said, "Hey, Haley. This is Jon. I was wondering if I could get your AOL Instant Messenger name. I'd love to talk."

After a really long pause, she said, "Okay."

I responded, "Okay, cool. Talk to you later."

I've already mentioned that I was ridiculously lame, right? I had no idea how to talk to her. I was too afraid to talk to her on the phone, so we just messaged back and forth on the computer. Today, people just text. Very reluctantly, she started talking to me more and more. We would "talk" for hours at a time. Before I knew it, it seemed like she had decided that I might not be so bad.

I was pretty persistent. Just as I watched the Olympics when I was younger and I knew I was going to get there one day, I knew as soon as I saw Haley that she was my girl. "She's going to be my girl forever," I thought. I eventually won her over, but I'm still not totally sure how. We started dating officially a few months later, and I would make the three-hour drive to Mckinney as many weekends as I could to visit her as she finished up her final year in high school.

Thankfully, Haley made the difficult decision to attend the University of Oklahoma. In a very Haley way, which is snarky and funny, she said to me, "Hey, I did not choose Oklahoma for you!"

I just returned a smile and an, "Uh huh…sure." I know she chose Oklahoma because she felt at home. It's where her parents and her family went, and she loved the gymnastics team. She most of all just loved the school, and although Stanford is a highly sought-after university, she decided she could be successful no matter where she went. I think she made a good choice. Haley became a multiple-time Big 12 conference balance beam champion, her team won the conference title twice, and she graduated at the top of her class with several letters of acceptance into medical schools. Not too shabby.

We had a great time together in college, and – hit the fast forward button – we've now been married over a decade. I look back on those days and laugh because I never thought I would find my wife as a freshman in college. It just kind of happened - I guess that's just the type of personality I have. I'm not even sure what I want until it's in front of me, then I go for it. I fell in love with Haley the moment I first looked at her, and I couldn't give it up. Luckily, even though it takes

Haley a bit longer to weigh things out and make decisions, she eventually came around. We continue to live a phenomenal life together … but only barely. She told me a few years back that on the night I asked her for her phone number, she almost gave me a fake one.

I'm pretty happy she didn't, and I did finally get that kiss.

My First
World Championship Meet

When I was a sophomore at Oklahoma, I qualified to participate in the 2006 World Championship meet – this would be my first time at Worlds! I had come a long way, not only in how I was performing but also in my attitude. Early on, my goal was to be the best all-arounder in the world and I was focused on what I could accomplish personally. When I got to college, that changed quickly as I realized the importance of competing as a team. When you compete for the USA, the emphasis on the team competition gets magnified many times over.

I had just won the NCAA title, so being invited to compete at Worlds was validation that I was now one of the best gymnasts in the country. Six guys made the World Championship team, and we were going to travel to Aarhus, Denmark for a month of competition.

In gymnastics, the World Championships is actually bigger than the Olympic Games in some ways. More teams and more athletes compete there. In fact, the Olympic field is narrowed down from that of the World Championships.

In 2006, there were over 30 teams, which meant *a lot* of competitors. I was pretty pumped, but in retrospect I realize that I was overly confident after winning a NCAA championship. I started feeling somewhat invincible and didn't think I could fail.

Because there are so many competitors at Worlds, the preliminary competition is split into several days and sessions. The worst session to compete in began early in the morning around 6:00 a.m. Unfortunately for team USA, we got the short end of the stick. We were headed to a 6:00 a.m. start time.

I didn't know it at the time, but preparation for full competition starting at 6:00 a.m. would be a nightmare. We now had to start waking up really early for our training sessions in addition to recovering from our jet lag. My entire workout schedule had to shift so that I could train my body to know what it was like to do full routines before I even felt awake. Due to our day one, session one competition, we would have to wake up at 3:00 a.m., eat breakfast, get ready, and start warming up for competition at 4:30 a.m. Yuck.

All of you current or retired gymnasts out there know that is NOT easy to do in the morning. You have to have enough time to wake up, warm up, stretch, and prepare to do all of the routines. Leading up to the competition I was hitting the gym at 4 a.m. with my coach, Mark Williams. and he kept drilling into me, "We gotta do this, and you have to be okay with feeling sluggish in the morning for competition. These are the cards we were dealt, and we have to play them." We tried a lot of different workouts. I tried to do routines and practice competitions, but I was struggling and having a hard time with just about everything at that time in the morning. There were several times we woke up and went to IHOP in the morning just to try to wake up, but I couldn't shake the early morning misery.

I remember being up at that early hour with my coach, and he said, "If you can't get used to this, Worlds is going to be embarrassing, so let's get it together." He was right. I decided I would be fine even though I couldn't get through my routines in training. I assumed that when the adrenaline kicked in during the actual competition, I would be good to go.

That couldn't have been farther from the truth.

We practiced those early morning training sessions for about a week and a half prior to the competition while in Denmark. I just *knew* everything would work out perfectly. I was going to lead my team. We would breeze through prelims and make it to finals. We would become one of the best teams in the world. We'd win medals, and I'd be an all-around top dog.

I didn't take the morning stuff seriously, and it bit me hard – so did being overly confident.

I ended up leading the team to the worst performance in U.S. history. We finished in 13th place, which was (and is) the lowest Team USA has ever finished at the elite level.

I fell on pommel horse, I fell on floor exercise, I fell twice on parallel bars, and twice on high bar. That means that I am also the only U.S. competitor in history to have fallen six times during one competition at World Championships. The only routines I didn't fall on that day were my ring routine and vault.

I won't make any excuses. While the team was relatively young and there were occasional mistakes from the other guys as well, I was the main reason we finished so poorly. I made mistakes on everything, and I ruined the team's chances of advancing.

Unfortunately, once the competition starts, the coaches are not allowed to swap athletes out unless there is an injury. They couldn't take me out of the meet, so I had to keep going and it was just a complete disaster. I remember being tired and frustrated, and I kept blaming the fact that we got stuck with this early morning session. The top eight teams from the preliminary round would get to compete again, but since we were in 13th place, we were done.

Our team put all this work in, went through miserable training sessions, flew across the world to Denmark – and boom, we were done. First day, first team out of the box, and it was over. The finality of it was cruel and abrupt.

The only guy on our team who performed well was Alexander Artemev, who was our pommel horse specialist. He did an amazing routine that morning and qualified to compete in the pommel horse finals where he won a bronze medal. I'll admit it - I was a really messy combination of proud and unbelievably jealous all at the same time. Other than Alex's success, Team USA had flopped. It was embarrassing. I was the guy who was supposed to be the rock star new kid on the block, and I let everyone down.

I remember people telling me how the administrators at USA gymnastics were upset, disappointed, and angry. I could also tell that my teammates were visibly frustrated with me and I felt like I had wasted my coaches' time. Honestly,

I didn't know if I would ever be trusted to compete internationally again. I guess if I had been blacklisted from the sport, I only had myself to blame.

It was a moment when I nearly decided to quit.

I remember sitting down and thinking that I would just finish out my collegiate career and hang up my gym bag. If I couldn't compete on the international stage and no one was going to trust me, why even try?

Then one day I had a meeting with my coach, Mark, and he asked me what I wanted to do. I pulled up my laptop and I sat there as we brainstormed. I just took notes. He spoke, then I told him how I was feeling, what we were doing, and what I thought I could do better.

I blamed my poor performance on everything but myself for a really long time until I suddenly realized I needed an attitude shift. Certainly there were aspects of my daily training habits that I needed to change. If I wanted to come back from the atrocious experience that I had, my mind and body needed an overhaul. I needed to figure out how to wrap my mind around a competition that big and what it would take to be successful. If I wanted to become an Olympian, I needed to figure out how to compete at the World Championships first.

I took pages and pages of notes, and by the time I was done I felt I had let go of a lot of my frustration and stopped feeling sorry for myself. I realized my goals were still doable, but I was going to have to sacrifice and suffer a little first.

I had two years left before the next Olympic Games, and I knew I needed to make some serious changes and commitments. I don't even know if my coach knows this, but after our meeting, I was still fuming. I couldn't believe this happened, and I wouldn't ever let it happen again. I told myself that I would prove to everyone – my team, my coaches, my country – that I was dependable and somebody who belonged on the international stage. I told myself at that moment that I was okay with suffering and being miserable because of the ridiculous amount of work that I was about to put into training. I was going to make the Olympic team, and I was willing to do whatever it took.

I think the 2006 World Championships was probably the most formidable experience of my whole career. I remember thinking about the Future Stars competition from back when I was a kid. I got last place and that had fueled me into many more years of being hungry for success. It was almost like I needed that reality check once again, but this time at the highest level.

I'm so thankful for the way God used that experience to reveal my weaknesses at that time. I was too confident in myself. I wasn't taking my career as seriously as I needed to be. I was humbled in the greatest (and most public) way possible in order to be made aware of the areas in my character that were lacking. Everything about me, mentally and physically, changed after that.

I started caring even more about how I could help my team because I never wanted my teammates to feel like this again. It was one thing to let myself down, but it was another thing to know that I had just ruined those guys' competition, too. I ruined it for them and for everyone else that had worked so hard to be there. This journey was no longer about me – it was about fighting harder for the men I stood next to.

I feel like I came to life as a result of that experience. Not only was I was training harder, but everything from A to Z changed – the way I was eating, the way I was sleeping, the way I was focused in the gym, and how I was treating my teammates. I made a huge shift and I became zeroed in on my newly sharpened vision. Thoughts like, "How do I get to the Olympics, and how do I help team USA rise to a position where this never happens again?" permeated my mind at all times.

I honestly wonder what kind of gymnast I would have been without that moment in 2006. I really don't think I would have ever accomplished what I ultimately did. I needed to fall flat on my face and to let everyone down, as bad as that sounds, or I think I would have just stayed lukewarm. Maybe I could have made the Olympic team, but I certainly don't believe I would have had the performance and the fire that I had for the next two years without that disaster. It was a necessary, brutally painful experience.

I had mentioned earlier that when I was 10 at the Future Stars, I finished 50th out of 50 kids, and then the following year when I was 11, I finished second. Well, I made the World Championship team in 2007, and in the typical pattern my career seems to follow, I once again experienced a 180 degree turnaround. The '07 world team placed fourth best, I finished fourth in the all-around, one of my teammates placed fourth on floor, another was fourth on rings, and another was fourth on pommel horse. Team USA didn't receive one medal in '07, but there wasn't another team that had as many top five finishes.

For me, to have the team rise from 13th place to fourth the following year, and for me to go from a disastrous individual performance to the fourth in the entire world was pretty exciting. I considered it a huge success!

I never said I made it easy on myself, though.

I began the competition on pommel horse, and I was in last place after that rotation (remember how I mentioned that pommel was my nemesis?). After the next event, I was still in last because of the hole I had dug for myself during the first rotation. My college coach, Mark Williams, was super encouraging and reminded me to focus on one routine at a time. He continually reminded me that, "It's not over until it's over!"

Slowly, I moved up in the standings after each event.

Finally, I made it to the last event sitting in 12th place. I knew I needed my best floor performance to have any hope for an individual medal. I delivered that performance and moved all the way up to 4th place, just two-tenths of a point away from the medals.

I would have liked being on the podium that day, but starting the race in last and finishing close to the front was still pretty special. It was noticed by everyone in the gymnastics world. I'll never forget the president of the Federation of International Gymnastics, Bruno Grandi, approaching me after the meet simply to tell me how bright of a future he saw for me and to say, "Well done." The three gymnasts who beat me were all World and Olympic champions, and I was right on their tails.

I was close, but I still had a lot of work to do.

The Pursuit of the
Olympic Dream

Although Team USA's performance at the 2007 Worlds was better than the year before, the five fourth-place finishes almost felt like a punch in the gut. The team finally had the satisfaction of knowing we were way better than 13th, but still none of us was an international medalist. That fired me up even more, and it was almost like a perfect storm was brewing. To be close, but not quite there the year before the Games gave me the fire and the edge I needed for the next year. The Olympic Games was in my crosshairs. I was totally locked on.

I had faith and believed that it was going to happen. I knew in my heart I was going to become an Olympian. But as the competition season leading up to the 2008 Olympics began, a lot started to go wrong. I started to really struggle on what was traditionally my best event – the high bar. I couldn't complete a clean high bar routine that year to save my life. I was performing a crazy advanced high bar routine that was a little extreme, but people really believed in it. For some reason though, competition after competition, I couldn't get through my routine without a major error or fall.

Even at the 2008 NCAA Championships when I was supposed to be nearing my peak, I fell on both parallel bars and high bar. We won the national title that year despite my performance because my teammates had my back. They fought like crazy for that win.

I'd had a really tumultuous year leading up to the Olympics, and it seemed to have no end in sight. The stress of carrying the weight of my goals was starting to take a toll. I was having such a hard time that my coach felt the need to bring in another coach to take a look at what was going on. His name was Dave Jusczyk.

Dave came to Oklahoma to work with me for about a week and showed me that the solution to my problems was simple: I needed to slow down. I was getting so worked up about every single little movement I was making that it was stressing me out. I was worried about the minutiae of every skill and routine, specifically on high bar, which meant I couldn't catch my major release elements the way I had been.

My college teammates used to call me X-Games because I threw a lot of high flying extreme release elements , but I felt like I was losing that nickname every time my body would hit the ground from another mistake. At this point, I struggled to execute like I knew I could, and it was driving me crazy.

As we got closer to the Olympics, I felt a constant level of adrenaline rushing through my body. I was too fast and too amped up to do anything with accuracy. Since I couldn't catch the bar in numerous competitions, we started taking all of the most difficult skills out of my routine. Because of that, the value of my routine was dropping quickly. I had been doing these routines for many years, but I couldn't get it together.

My time with Dave Jusczyk was productive. During that week, he worked with me on how to slow down, relax, and focus on the big picture instead of getting stressed out about every little thing. Soon after, I went to the U.S. Championships, which was a two-day competition. Doing well at this meet was the starting place to qualifying for the Olympics, and then the Olympic Trials would be up next. Olympic Trials was also a two-day event. Between these two meets, I had four chances to prove myself on all six events.

I did four high bar routines leading up to the Olympics, and I only completed one of them cleanly without a fall.

Although I had worked tirelessly on fixing my performance issues, I still hadn't escaped the hole I was stuck in. I just couldn't stay on the bar, and this created a pretty big problem. When you only hit 25% of your routines, the selection committee and all the coaches have a real dilemma regarding the selection process. They knew I had a lot of potential and that I could be great, but did they really want to put potential on the team instead of the sure thing? I know if I were them, it would have been tough to choose the kid who hadn't proven himself to be clutch under pressure.

Luckily, the rest of my gymnastics helped round out the case for putting me on the team. Five out of my six routines were on fire, and I did well enough to win Olympic Trials. I earned that spot on the Olympic team in 2008 and the dream I'd had for 12 years was squarely in front of me.

I was thrilled, but I was running out of time to fix the problems.

Beijing!

When I qualified for the Olympics in Beijing, China, I was finally where I felt I was meant to be. I was born to be here, and I had been dreaming about this moment since watching the 1996 Games on television.

Gymnastics at the Olympics is broken into five days of competition, which are spread out over a two-week period. Competitions include team qualifications, team finals, all-around finals, and two days of individual event finals. As a team, we were favored to finish at the top because Paul and Morgan Hamm had just come out of retirement. Paul and Morgan were twin brothers who were on both the 2000 and 2004 Olympic teams. They both came out of retirement when the US team was struggling as a whole, and they saw an opportunity to help in a big way. They came back in their usual, phenomenal fashion and both made the 2008 Olympic team. At that time, Paul Hamm was the current Olympic all-around champion! With Morgan also being one of the best, we knew this would be a huge boost for Team USA.

I couldn't believe it – I was on the Olympic team with a couple of my heroes. I looked up to these guys, and I knew it would be very cool to experience the Olympics with them. It was also nice to know that we had a legitimate shot at winning a medal!

However, athletic tragedy struck. In a sport like gymnastics, you never know when something crazy will happen. Paul broke his hand a couple months before the Games, and after a successful surgery but slower-than-desired recovery process, he made the decision to sit out. Fortunately for the rest of us, Olympic and World Teams are composed of the roster of competing athletes (in this case, six) in addition to three reserve athletes on hand ready to jump into action. One of the reserve athletes in Beijing happened to be my older teammate from childhood, Raj Bhavsar, and he was selected to take Paul's position.

Raj and I weren't really that close as friends before being on the Olympic team. Raj was five years older than me and we hadn't ever been on a competitive assignment together. He was already in high school when I came to Cypress Academy of Gymnastics as a little twerp, and being the phenomenal gymnast that he was, Raj was always one of those guys that I looked up to. Honestly, I wanted to be Raj. He was one of the most exciting, quick, and powerful gymnasts in the world, and I loved his unorthodox style of gymnastics. Raj had also battled through a lot to experience this moment of Olympic glory. Back in 2004, Raj had been selected as the reserve athlete for that Olympic team as well.

Now, I want to make something very clear. To come so close to your dream, the same dream you've had since you were a small child, to train and travel with the team, but not be able to compete … that's really, really difficult for an athlete. Our reserve athletes (or "alternates") take on that position with pride and a sense of responsibility, and are absolutely the unsung heroes of their respective teams. Nonetheless, Raj had decided after the Olympics in 2004 to retire from his gym career with a pretty sour taste in his mouth. In my opinion, Raj's comeback after retirement in 2004 to being one of the top US gymnasts in the country in 2008 is one of the greatest sports stories ever. But after all of that, he ended up as an alternate in 2008 for the second time. It was a difficult thing to watch him process and experience. Needless to say, the mixture of sadness for Paul and elation for Raj that I felt when my coach called to tell me Paul was relinquishing his spot and Raj would be stepping in is difficult to describe!

But, we had just lost the current Olympic all-around champion; that's an enormous shock to a team! He was our leader, and thoughts of "How do we do this?" and "Can we do this?" began to creep in. Fortunately, people still believed in us, and we were excited to have Raj. And hey, we still had Morgan Hamm. We believed we could medal, but knew it would be very difficult.

Unfortunately, our problems with injury continued once we arrived in Beijing. During a pre-meet training session, Morgan started having some ankle issues and was experiencing quite a bit of pain. He had been having some difficulty with his ankle leading up to the Games, but he thought he could overcome it. Because of the pain, though, he really started to struggle on what was traditionally one of his best events, the floor exercise. The day before we were to compete in the preliminary round, Morgan did a floor routine and completely destroyed his ankle. While doing a skill called a double layout, he ran down the floor like normal, jumped in the air, did two flips in the stretched position that we call "layout," and dropped like a rock. His feet crunched hard into the ground. We could see that as soon as he landed, he was laying on the floor with tears in his eyes – not because he was in pain, which of course he was – but because he knew he was done. As he stood up, he limped over to us and he said, "Guys, I'm sorry. I can't go on."

That was a really emotional time for the team. We had already lost Paul, but now we knew we'd lost his brother Morgan, too. I'm not exactly the most emotional guy in the world; in fact, my teammates in college used to give me a hard time about that fact that I never cried (about anything … ever). But there were two times in my athletic career when the emotions did hit me hard, and neither of them occurred because of personal performance or injury. Both were due to losing a teammate I cared deeply about to injury.

The first occurred in 2003 when I was in high school and had the opportunity to compete at the Pan American Games in Santo Domingo, Dominican Republic. The day before we competed, my teammate, Sho Nakamori, ran down the vault runway to do a vault called a Yurchenko double full.

Without being too graphic, Sho's vault went something like this: he ran down the vault runway, launched into the air, did his vault, and came back down on the side of his leg. All the people training and preparing for competition heard a *snap*. To me it sounded like a tree branch breaking in half. Sho hit the ground so hard that he broke his femur. At that moment, we knew that Sho was going to have to be flown home for surgery, and that we would be without our teammate. I remember being an emotional wreck because I felt badly for Sho and I knew how badly he wanted to be with us. We all fought hard to compete well for him at that competition.

The same emotions poured out of me when Morgan had to leave Beijing because of his ankle injury. First, I wanted so badly to be able to take the pain away from Morgan and have him lead our team the way I knew he could. Second, I knew first hand how hard he had worked to be there! I couldn't stand the thought of him being so close to competing but going home instead. Third, I wondered how our team would be able to move on. We went from being a powerhouse group to having nobody with any Olympic experience on our team. To top it off, our alternate athletes knew in the back of their minds that they had to step into the shoes of arguably two of the greatest gymnasts the United States has ever had – not exactly an easy task.

Who was going to replace Morgan, though? We had started out with three reserve athletes. After Paul's injury and Raj's replacement of him on the team, we had Dave Durante and Alexander Artemev left – both incredible guys, both ready to go. Now only one of them would be left off the team; that made our difficult situation so much worse! Now, the selection committee responsible for choosing the team had to come together and decide who to put on the team the day before we were supposed to compete. Ultimately, they selected Alex because he was a specialist on the pommel horse and that was our team's weakest event.

At that point, after losing the Hamm twins, everyone in the media ripped us apart. On Twitter and Facebook, which were relatively new at the time, people were saying things like, "Oh great, Jonathan Horton is at the helm of this team." I could feel their eyes rolling all the way from China.

It's funny now, but it wasn't at the time.

There was an article written about us at the time that I will never forget. It was from a writer with the Associated Press who said our team looked like a bunch of backup players and that we had no shot at winning a medal. It felt true, but we had still made an Olympic team! We didn't deserve to be called backups and we certainly didn't want to hear it the night before competition began. We took it hard, and I remember that we were all super nervous. Out of the six guys who made the Olympic team, none of us had ever stepped onto the floor at an Olympic Games, and we had no idea what the moment would feel like. It would have been nice to have someone there to tell us, "Guys, I've been here before and it's going to be okay." This was different than any other meet any of us had ever been in. The hype, the arenas, the athletes, the media, the fans, and the atmosphere were all so overwhelming.

Imagine sitting at a table, enjoying a meal in the Olympic village and trying to relax when you notice that at the other end of it is LeBron James. Usain Bolt is sitting at a table to your left, and directly behind you is Michael Phelps.

That happened.

In moments like that, reality really settled in.

The nerves were unlike anything I've ever experienced, and to know that the rest of the world didn't believe in us at all was a scary thing. We were just a rag tag group of guys that was thrown together at the last minute to go compete at the freakin' Olympics.

The night before we competed, we all got together as a team. Kevin Tan, our team captain, called us together. We sat in a circle out on the balcony of our apartment in the middle of the Olympic village, and just started pouring out our feelings.

Some guys admitted to being scared, others had doubts about whether or not they could compete. One of our guys, because of Morgan Hamm's injury, was being forced to fill in and do a floor routine that he hadn't done more than a handful of times in the past year because of his own injuries.

And Raj, who can be a real emotionally intense guy, says, "Guys, I don't know if I can do this. I feel like I'm gonna puke."

In fact, I even told the guys, "I don't wanna fall anymore. I can't let this team down. I can't afford to choke again."

It was actually a pretty great moment. Collectively, we all had so many fears and doubts, but there was something comforting about seeing everyone be vulnerable and knowing we weren't alone. That night on the balcony we truly became the 2008 Olympic team. More so than knowing we had trained hard and shared the grind together as a team, we realized how much we cared about each other. We realized that we were brothers in this.

If we were betting on poker that night, it would have been the equivalent of pushing every chip to the middle and asking each other, "Who's taking the bet?" It was game time.

That was a defining moment.

That night I slept like a baby. I wasn't alone, and I had brothers who had my back no matter what happened in competition.

The next day, we walked out onto the Olympic floor in our red, white and blue, as the electricity of the arena filled us with energy. The host country of China did the Olympics very well. There were 40,000 people there, and that venue was one of the most beautiful things I've ever seen. The entire team paced back and forth as we soaked in every moment, waiting for our turn to compete.

I'm a man of faith in God. Right before we were official-ly introduced to the spectators, I circled the guys up and I said, "Hey look, I know not everyone here shares my beliefs, but can I say a prayer for the team?" And everybody was so amped up and nervous that they said, "Yeah, man, we'll do anything. We'll take anything right now, let's say this prayer."

So we got together, bowed our heads, and I said a prayer over the team. We've since laughed ourselves to tears think-ing about those first moments in the arena because they can be defined by a single word: panic.

We were all 100% in, willing to do whatever it took to succeed, and even in that moment it made us chuckle. I'm not sure if we were laughing because we were enjoying our-selves or if the amount of desperation we felt about not fail-ing was comical. It didn't matter. We were freaking out, but at the same time, our moment was perfect. We marched out into that arena with our heads up, thinking to ourselves that we didn't care what happened or how we finished as long as we did it with pride. No one believed in us but us, and we were going to make our country proud. Whether we nailed our routines or fell all over the place, we were going to walk out of that arena as Olympians - as champions - knowing that we were some of the best gymnasts in the entire world. We got to compete at the Olympics, represent our country with our flag across our chests, and we realized that even being there was an honor.

We set all of our fears aside. It was time to go for it.

We started out on rings, and as soon as each guy landed his dismount, we said to him, "Hey, congratulations bro. You're officially an Olympian!" You could see the smile on everyone's face, and the energy within our team grew. I was the second to last guy up on rings and I couldn't wait to land my dismount and have my team look at me and say, "Hey man, you're now a real Olympian!" When I landed that dismount, I walked off the podium and I said, "Give it to me guys, tell it to me!"

And they did.

The pride I felt about what I'd accomplished – no matter what I did after that moment – was unforgettable. I was an Olympian – forever.

The energy and the love that we had for one another carried to the next event, and the next event, and the next event. After our first day, the team preliminary competition, was over, Alexander Artemev and I had qualified for the all-around finals, I qualified into the high bar final, and our team finished in sixth place out of the twelve teams that competed. A lot of people were surprised that we were even in the top eight, which was the qualifying mark to advance to the next day. Needless to say, we were pumped. We certainly cele-brated the excitement from our first official Olympic com-petition, but we had some even bigger tasks ahead and we wanted to keep our eyes on the prize.

Two days after the qualifying round, we were set to com-pete in the team finals. The best eight teams in the entire world were about to put their best three gymnasts up on each event. And with gold, silver, and bronze medals on the line, there was absolutely zero room for error. We started out on rings again, and as a team, something magical happened. We quickly realized that day was going to be special. Nobody was making any mistakes! Routine after routine we got bet-ter, and no one missed a set. Our strength was in the fact that we had nothing to lose, and we didn't care what any-one thought. We didn't care about what any other athletes, coaches, judges, fans, or families were thinking. During that competition, the ultimate competition for any gymnast in the world, it was simply about me and my five teammates living our dream together, and it felt like no one else was around. We were on fire.

I had what felt like a perfect day. And honestly? I've nev-er spoken to another gymnast who has had one. I'm the only person that I know of that's ever hit every single routine and stuck every single possible landing.

I did my ring routine and stuck my dismount.

I vaulted and stuck my landing.

Parallel bars? Nailed it.

High bar? Perfect.

I competed on floor, and stuck all five of my tumbling passes – something I'd never even done in training.

I've never seen another gymnast do that. The only analogy I can think of is that it was like being a baseball pitcher and throwing a perfect game, or maybe bowling a perfect 300. But even those two scenarios happen more often than a perfect gymnastics meet. I had people come up to me that said, "Dude, that was the greatest performance we've ever seen. How'd you do it?"

Honestly? I have no idea. I felt like I couldn't have messed up if I tried. When I was in the air, it was like I was in this "flow" and that I had complete control over every aspect of my body. I felt like I was able to perfectly control how high I jumped, how fast I spun, and like my muscles refused to fatigue. I had never felt so comfortable.

Whatever was happening to me must have been contagious, because while my other five teammates weren't perfect, they were darn close.

One of my favorite moments from the entire Olympics happened on high bar. For team USA, high bar was our bread and butter. In spite of the struggles I was having in preparation for the games, our team was still power packed on that event. Joseph Hagerty was up first, which is a situation that's nerve racking on any event. But in typical Joey fashion, he sailed through his routine like a pro and put up our first big score. It was my turn.

The lineup format for gymnastics at the Olympics is a little daunting. For a six-man team, as it was back then, each team is required to select its best five gymnasts in the preliminary round to compete on each event. The best four scores from those five would count toward the final score. This means that each team has one throw away card on every event. However, if your team was fortunate enough to qualify into the finals, the medal round, things would change. In that situation each team picks its three best gymnasts on each event and all three scores must count toward the final team tally. That means there is *zero* room for error. Every single person has to do his job, under pressure, in front of the bright lights and cameras, with judges in his face, and billions of people watching at home. You. Cannot. Fall.

Because of that format, in my opinion, the high bar is the scariest event to perform. It's such a wild event with so many risky skills, and it made my heart beat 200 beats per minute in anticipation of my routine.

My coach walked up behind me, lifted me to the 10-foot-high steel bar, and I started swinging. For one of the only times all season, I caught every release element and did the hardest dismount of anyone in the world. I flew off the bar in full speed and turned over a triple twisting double layout and stuck my landing. The crowd went berserk, and we all laughed because the craziest guy on our team hadn't even performed yet! My score came up as the crowd was still cheering, and Justin Spring, our third and final guy, approached the bar.

Like I said, Justin was a lunatic on high bar. Nobody swung faster and flew higher than him, which is why no other team in the world had higher blood pressure than we did at the time. He made us extremely nervous because he lived on the edge during every moment of the routine. Justin jumped up to the bar to begin, and within a matter of seconds, our team had our hands over our faces, peeking between our fingers as the crowd stood in disbelief, shouting "oohs" and "ahhs" at the madness they were witnessing. After flying through the air in what appeared to be a reckless fashion for 30 seconds, Justin wound up for a triple backflip to finish his routine. Of course, he stuck it. If you go back and watch the BBC version of the Olympic coverage, one of the British commentators shouted after Justin's routine, "He landed on a patch of glue!" They were just as excited as we were, and almost everyone in the crowd was on their feet.

High bar was the fourth event and we're high-fiving and cheering each other on, having the time of our lives. Here we were in China, where 90% of the fans in the crowd are Chinese, and we got a standing ovation and a "USA" chant from the entire crowd of 40,000 people. It was bananas! We were looking around asking each other, "Can you believe this?" At that moment, we weren't sure if we would win the meet that day, but we knew we had won the love of the crowd. The moment reminded me of a line from one of my favorite movies, "Gladiator." Proximo, the gladiator trader, looks at Maximus, the mighty gladiator, and says, "Win the crowd, and you will win your freedom." After high bar was over, it didn't really matter what happened the rest of the time we were there. We were free from any stress, anxiety, or worry about the final results. We won the love of the crowd and the people watching around the world.

I had never witnessed anything like that before – a standing ovation from what is usually a fairly hostile crowd. If you know anything about gymnastics, you know that it's one of the most popular sports in China. They love their gymnastics there, but the fans stood up and cheered for us. I remember looking over at the Chinese gymnasts, and it looked like they were thinking "What in the world? Why are all of our fans cheering on Team USA?"

After that fourth event, we were in first place – no joke, we were winning the meet! China and Japan were the two most dominant teams in the world, and we were beating them going into our last two events. I think everyone was just as shocked as we were.

Unfortunately, our two remaining events, floor and pommel horse, were among our weakest. We put up our three floor routines and we survived. Again, I did the best routine of my life. Justin Spring, the guy who just the night before was freaking out and didn't know if he could get through a floor routine, performed really well. It wasn't his best, but the relief on his face said it all.

Then we went to pommel horse… bum bum bummmmm (cue dark scary music with ominous lighting)!

Pommel horse is a hard enough event by itself, but now we had to do it last, at the Olympics, during a three up, three count competition format where any mistake is detrimental to your final team's score. Oh yeah, and we had an Olympic medal on the line that nobody thought was possible for us to win. Against all odds, we were in silver medal contention – no pressure, guys.

We didn't fall apart, but we certainly didn't have spectacular performances. Our first guy up, Kevin Tan, made a few mistakes but stayed on and fought with every single ounce of strength he had to finish the routine. Second up, Raj did the same thing and battled through without a fall. If you ask Raj today what he felt in that moment before starting his routine, he will give the most ridiculous and hilarious answer you've ever heard. I won't ruin it, so if you're reading this, you'll just have to find a way to contact him and ask him yourself. Don't drink anything before asking or it'll come out of your nose.

In my opinion, one of the craziest stories from the Games that didn't receive enough attention was the role of our pommel horse anchor, Alexander Artemev. Because Alex was one of our reserve athletes, he was brought onto the team specifically for pommel horse. He didn't do another routine that day in finals. Since pommel horse was our last event, he had to sit around all day and wait ... and wait ... and wait. Sure, he'd warmed up before the meet started, but then he sat around for two and a half hours before he could perform. Needless to say, Alex had a lot of time to think about the possibility of having to anchor the team. Depending on where we were standing when we got to pommel, he could have to do the greatest routine of his life – under pressure, last guy up, on the last event.

If you're looking for a good non-gymnastics analogy for the situation Alex was in, here is the best I can come up with. Alex was our Super Bowl kicker. He had one job, and that job was to kick a 55-yard field goal with one second left on the clock to win the game. Plus, none of his team knew if he was feeling good because he hadn't kicked a single ball the whole game.

Okay, back to gymnastics. Because Alex joined the team late, he hadn't gotten to practice in the Olympic arena as much as the rest of us. Morgan had still been on the team during our practice sessions. As a reserve athlete, Alex was in another arena in Beijing and was not allowed to train with us. Alex squeaked through a routine in prelims, but that isn't really enough time to get a feel for the equipment. Every arena has a different feel and it's important for us to adjust to that and the new equipment. The rest of us had competed on the apparatus and practiced on it enough to know what to expect. However, this was his second time on the pommel horse, and he was going to have to go last when he was cold and not warmed up.

At this point, before Alex's routine, we had dropped back into third place.

Still, winning a bronze medal after everything we'd gone through would be truly unbelievable. Team Germany was nipping at our heels for that bronze, and Alex had to come through under pressure. If he fell, we wouldn't win a medal. If he nailed his routine, we would shock the gymnastics world.

He raised his hand, got up on the pommel horse, and started his routine. That was the most terrifying moment of my entire career – way more so than when I was competing myself. My heart was pounding a billion miles an hour as I sat off to the side. I had zero control over the moment, and it was terrible. I was over in a corner, and I had the hood of my Team USA jacket over my head quietly saying, "Please Alex, please, please, please, please, please stay on this pommel horse."

I could identify with exactly how Alex felt in that moment. One of the reasons he hadn't made the 2008 Olympic Team out right (remember, he was a reserve athlete first) was because he was a little like me. His best event was pommel horse, but he had fallen on it three out of four days at the U.S. Championships and Olympic Trials. But …

Not! This! Time!

Alex was known for his style and difficulty on pommel horse. Skill after skill he floated effortlessly above the pommel horse. He flared his way up and down the horse, balanced on one pommel for what seemed like an eternity, and never once lost control of a skill. 100% CLUTCH. When he landed, I jumped ten feet in the air. I swear I could have slam dunked a basketball that day with how high I was jumping. The rest of the team went crazy, and everyone in the crowd was losing their minds. He had one of the most complicated and difficult pommel horse routines in the world, and for him to step up and stone cold tear it up – insane!

Alex's score flashed on the big screen in the middle of the arena, and Team USA, a bunch of guys that everyone doubted, became the Olympic bronze medal team.

The Moment That Changed Everything

Team bronze was monumental, but my Olympics wasn't over. I had qualified for the high bar finals, and there's a long, wild history of how I arrived there – a place I never, in a million years, thought I would be.

High bar can be brutal because of how high flying it is. If not executed correctly, it can be dangerous. I definitely had my share of bumps and bruises during my personal high bar journey.

When I was eight years old, I did my best to learn the most foundational skill on high bar called a "giant." Giants are completed when you circle around the bar on nothing but your hands. My coach at my first gym, Jim Culhane, was teaching me how to do giants on a strap bar. With strap bars, you're anchored to the metal bar with special straps on your wrists. This makes it impossible to accidentally fly off. My coach stood there and helped me understand how to manipulate my body in order to swing around the bar.

It took me a while to figure out how to do it, but once I got it, I discovered that it was one of my favorite things in the world. Circling around the bar over and over again until I felt like I was going to puke? I just loved it. I was still strapped onto the bar while I was learning, so again, I was relatively safe.

One day, Coach looked at me and said, "All right, let's get out of the straps. Put your grips on and we'll go do some giants on the real high bar.

I thought, "Oh no. We're going to the real bar." The training wheels, so to speak, were coming off.

I was a little kid and trusted my coach. I jumped up to the bar and I had to decide which kind of giant I wanted to do, a forward giant or a backward giant. I was better at the forward ones, so he told me to start with those. Coach stood up on a spotting block, I jumped up to handstand, and I made my first circle around the bar. As my body approached the bottom of the bar, though, I panicked and let go. My coach wasn't able to react fast enough to catch me. Honestly, I don't think any coach could have caught me because it all happened so fast.

In gymnastics, we call what I ended up doing a "scorpion" landing. I landed with my chin on the mat, my feet flew over my head, and my butt nearly touched the back of my head. It hurt my back so badly and I vividly remember not being able to breathe for a moment. My dad was up in the viewing area watching, and he ran out on the floor because he thought I had seriously injured myself. Luckily, nothing serious happened, but I was officially terrified of high bar. I had hurt myself on my first attempt at learning a giant, and my coach told me, "We're going to back off of this because you're not ready."

After a few months, I started slowly making progress toward the giant. I had developed a mental block from being so scared, so it took a really long time. I kept imagining myself falling and hurting my back again, and I couldn't get the moment out of my head.

When I was nine and moved to Cypress Academy for my training, my coaches, Tom Meadows and Aaron Basham, noticed pretty quickly that I was horrible at high bar. My giants were horrendous, I had terrible technique, and I was terrified. Every necessary movement on high bar took me forever to figure out. There were so many skills that other kids would learn in a few days or weeks, but would take me months if not years to figure out. It was extremely frustrating.

When I was a pre-teen, I was trying to learn some of the little intricate moves on high bar that my teammates like Chris Brooks, Raj, and some others were doing. They were all in the gym performing these cool tricks using a bunch of precise movements where you need to move your hand back and forth to spin around. I couldn't figure out how to do them. They were difficult, scary, and I always felt like I was about to fly off of the bar unexpectedly. Slowly but surely, though, I started making progress toward learning a skill or two.

I watched a ton of video of the '96 Olympics during that time. I always loved learning from and studying my heroes. Somehow, those little intricate skills scared me, but the way the best of the best did high flying release moves on the high bar didn't look scary at all. That looked fun! I remember asking my coach, Tom, if I could learn a particular release skill, and he was extremely hesitant. I decided to take it upon myself to go over to the foam pit and start learning it by myself without getting permission. Chris Brooks followed suit, and we started trying to learn these moves together.

Right about that time, a switch flipped in my brain. I suddenly lost my fear of nearly everything, almost to the point where my teammates thought I was a little loony! I really don't know what happened, but I wanted to try everything.

When I was 11, I learned my first release element on high bar called a Gienger. It's a back flip with a half turn, after which you catch the bar. I remember catching my first one and thinking, "Oh man! That was fun. I want to do these all day!" I got comfortable with it, and I decided that I wanted to scrap all the other tricks these guys were doing and focus on being the guy who throws a ton of release elements. I had gotten rid of a lot of my fear of the intricate skills, but I still wasn't any good at them.

Back then, most gymnasts did one release move – two at the most. Any time you let go of the bar, there's a chance you won't catch it! There's just a lot to it - if you don't let go of the bar at the perfect time, or if you don't bend the bar the right way, it can all go horribly wrong. Release skills require a lot of precision, but I decided that if I could really commit to this, I could do four, maybe five in one routine. It would mean I'd have a pretty unique high bar routine, even if I struggled with everything else.

At that moment, without even knowing it, I began to pave my own way through the sport. One of the most recognizable releases in the sport is called a Kovacs. Back then a Kovacs was an iconic move because if a gymnast could pull it off, he would be considered one of the best. A lot of people do them now, but that was not the case 20 years ago. A Kovacs is essentially a double backflip over the high bar that you have to place in the perfect spot so you can grab the bar after the second flip. To execute it properly, you swing around the bar as fast as you can, let go, do a double back flip, then grab the bar.

When I was 13 years old, I told myself that I was going to learn a Kovacs. I wanted to be the youngest person to ever do it. To learn it, I started watching as many videos as I could find of people performing the skill. This was the moment that I became more than just a gymnast, I became a true student of the sport. I began studying the way different guys created power by pulling on the bar, the way they pushed it, and the way they could create massive explosive height for a big trick.

I told my coach, "I'm going to learn this," and he said, "No, you're not."

He told me, "If you want, you can go play with learning how to move the bar to create force and power."

There was a thing we did in gymnastics called a tap. You pull up on the bar, then pull down, and you can really move the bar when a tap is performed properly.

Coach told me I could work on the tap for as long as I wanted, but he wouldn't allow me to let go of the bar and try a Kovacs for a long time. So that's what I did. I worked on the tap, and I tried to learn how to manipulate the bar, move it, and create force and power. One day I decided it was time. I went over to the high bar that was over our foam pit and I told myself, "I'm going for it. I'm just going to figure it out." I started doing what I'd practiced for a few months and I threw myself over the high bar. I survived the double back flip, but I wasn't even close to catching it. Everybody asked me, "*What* are you doing?" I said, "Hey guys, I'm learning a Kovacs."

Given the fact that I hadn't gravely injured myself on my first few attempts, my coaches decided to let me keep trying. I just kept doing them over and over again. Every single time I did it, I got a little bit closer, and a little bit closer, and a little bit closer. Then on the second day of trying them, I caught the bar. Everybody in the gym went crazy and a few of my teammates told me I was insane. In hindsight, they were probably right. I was 13 years old doing one of the biggest tricks in the sport. I caught a Kovacs! I remember thinking, "Yeah, this is it. Game on."

From that point on, I wanted to learn every variation of a Kovacs I could think of, and there were quite a few of them.

When I was 14, I started to catch them more consistently, and I wondered if I could add a full twist to it. So I tried that and I and caught it my very first day. Then I wondered if I could fly high enough over the bar to do it with my legs straight in the laid-out position. I started practicing the laid-out Kovacs, which took me a while and was the toughest to learn, but I finally got the hang of it after four months.

Then I looked over at my coach one day and said, "How crazy would it be if I did a laid-out Kovacs, a full twisting Kovacs, and a traditional Kovacs all in one routine?" I think he finally saw how crazy and how serious I was, so he said, "You know what? Maybe that's what Jonathan Horton is meant to do. Let's start training it all."

No one else in the entire world was doing a routine like this because there was simply too much risk involved. Even for me, this routine was pretty unsuccessful in the beginning. I couldn't catch all three in a row, but day after day I just kept trying. With my inability to do the more intricate skills, I didn't have many other options. I was committed to mastering what I was good at.

The other things I got really good at doing were dismounts. No one else could dismount off of high bar the way I could. Since I was spending so much time learning the Kovacs tap technique, I learned how to manipulate the bar very well. That made it much easier to learn how to do a huge dismount!

In a relatively short period of time, I learned a lot of really extreme, unique elements. It didn't come without backlash from others, but my personal coach had come around to my style by then. The administrators and some of the head coaches of the National Team were keeping a close eye on what I was doing. They said things like, "This isn't going to work, he needs to go back and focus on the other stuff that isn't so risky." They kept saying over and over again that consistent, successful completion of a routine like this would be impossible. I was told that I was too inconsistent; I was told there was no way I'd ever be able to do a routine like this under pressure. They felt I should stop learning it altogether. Keep in mind that I wasn't hearing this from just one person – it was many - and some of them were big decision makers in the sport of gymnastics. I had just started showing some potential and they seemed to be fighting it hard.

I started attempting the routine at different small competitions, and I would fall on it the majority of the time. I would get a big cheer from the crowd for trying, but I couldn't finish it successfully... yet. At one point, I did question the reality of being able to successfully complete the routine. I wondered if I was wasting my time falling so much, but I loved how the crowd loved it! It seemed way more fun to go perform and entertain people than to focus on not falling on an easier routine. Obviously I didn't want to fall, but even when I did, it was a huge adrenaline rush.

I just kept trying. I was committed, and I wasn't turning back. I told myself that I wasn't going to do what I wasn't good at just because it was the more traditional path. I'd keep pressing forward with what I was capable of regardless of what anyone else thought. I knew it was radical, but it had to be possible. Maybe there just hadn't been anyone else who had committed to it long term like I was willing to?

Fast forward a few years to Junior Nationals when I was in high school. I went for my wild routine in front of all of the college recruiters, and I absolutely nailed it. I did all three of my major releases with a double twisting, double backflip dismount, and I stuck my landing. Every single one of the college coaches stood up after my routine and walked over to my coach. I didn't know what they were talking about at the time, but they were telling my coach, "We have to have this kid."

It took me a long time to learn that routine, and even after that moment at junior nationals, I continued to be in-consistent. I struggled for many years, and I won't deny the fact that I had a really difficult time dealing with the routine under pressure. The experienced coaches in the sport were right. They were right for a long time. I couldn't do the rou-tine under pressure, it was extremely inconsistent, and there was nothing smart about it. I knew it was dangerous and wild, but it was my only path. I had to make the decision and commit 100% – this was what I was going to do.

By the time I became an Olympian in 2008, I was a multiple time junior, senior, and collegiate national champion on high bar. It only took a decade of constant work.

As I mentioned a few chapters ago, the season leading up to the Olympic Games was full of struggle on high bar. My coach and I decided to water down my routine a bit to ensure successful completion during the team preliminary competition at the Olympics. Our strategy worked, and I completed it beautifully that night. I had removed the laid-out Kovacs, and because I was doing a devalued routine, I didn't think I was going to be one of the top performers. Somehow, I still finished in seventh place after prelims. The top eight finishers qualify to high bar finals, and I was one of them. I was pumped!

The moment of truth was at hand. I had a shot at winning a gold medal and becoming an Olympic champion. Should I go all out, or play it smart and see what happens?

I said to my coaches and teammates, "I've got a wild idea. What if I just throw it all in? Do every single release move I can possibly think of in one routine for the finals? I'll put the laid-out Kovacs back in the routine, I'll add another big release element that I haven't performed in competition, and I'll do the hardest dismount in the world."

Most of my career I did a double twisting, double layout dismount. At the Olympics, I decided to do a triple twisting double. No one else in the meet was doing it. Not one person.

The other skill I wanted to add was the Cassina, which is a laid-out Kovacs combined with a full twist. I believe only one other person had done it at this point – that was a guy named Igor Cassina (yes, he did it first, and yes, he got to name it). He just so happened to be the 2004 Olympic gold medalist on high bar. So I told my coach, "Hey, I'm going to do that skill plus add all the other ones that I used to do. I'll risk falling, but I know that I'll have a chance to win. I know I've never done this routine before; I've never even *thought* about it before, but I'm going to go for it. I don't just want to participate in the finals on high bar, I want to at least have a chance at gold.

And my coach said, "No way. Uh-uh, not going to happen. You've only done the Cassina in competition a few times and you fell on all of them."

To his credit, he probably legitimately thought I'd hurt myself. I had successfully completed the skill only a few times, even in training! He told me, "It's too wild - too extreme. Just go do what you know how to do, land your dismount, and be excited about the fact that you're an Olympic finalist on high bar!"

I heard what he was saying. I understood it. But I wasn't okay with it. I wasn't going to accept that I was simply a participant. I wanted to win, and I had nothing to lose at this point.

At this point, I had tried this routine in the warm-up facility for several days before the competition. All the other athletes, including the other seven guys that would be competing in the final AND 2004 Olympic gold medalist Igor Cassina, were there too. I tried this insane routine many times and fell all over the place. I kept "splatting" (yes, that's the technical term) and I couldn't catch the full twisting laid out Kovacs. I knew what everyone was thinking: "What is this stupid American doing? Is he trying to hurt himself before the final?" My coach was shaking his head. In hindsight, I think he was probably embarrassed. "Stop. Do your normal routine," he said.

Finally, there was a brief moment of hope in the warm-up facility when I got through the entire routine. When I got to my dismount, though, I was completely exhausted and landed right on my side. I wasn't even close to landing it. I had never completed a routine that had so many difficult elements, and I was beyond fatigued by the end of it. At that moment, since I did technically get through the routine, I saw one of the Chinese coach's ears perk up. He went over to our translator and the translator approached my coach. The Chinese coach was wanting to know what the start value of the routine would be if I completed it. My coach told him the answer, and he walked back to his own team. It seemed like they were wondering, "What if this silly American can actually pull this off?"

I think that day in the warm up gym made their wheels turn, because on the day of competition, the Chinese gymnast added several elements to his routine to increase the difficulty. Back in those days, it was pretty uncommon in gymnastics to change your routine at the Olympics. Traditionally, you go to the Olympics because you've trained the same routine over and over again, and you keep that routine because you know what to expect. You flip on the autopilot and go. To change a routine at that point in the competition would be unprecedented.

The Chinese coach saw the routine I was attempting, and he told his athlete to try something new. I think they figured that I was getting close to successfully completing it. I don't know if the rest of the athletes in there took me seriously, but that one Chinese coach was wise enough to know that it would only take one time of me getting through that crazy routine to throw an Olympic sized wrench into everyone else's plan.

I like to think I got into their heads a little.

After five days of waiting and contemplating what I would do, the day of the competition finally arrived!

Nothing was set in stone, even up to the moment that I raised my hand to do my routine. At that time, my coach asked, "Are you sure you don't want to do your normal routine? Go and perform what you know how to do?"

"You've been so good since you arrived in Beijing," he said. "You haven't made a single mistake. Just do your normal routine."

I know why he said it. I know he just wanted me to finish my Olympic experience on a high note. He loved me and cared for me deeply, and we'd been through so much together. He didn't want to see me fall in front of billions of people and leave Beijing disappointed.

But in my mind, there was no way I could leave Beijing disappointed. I was already a bronze medalist and everything else was icing on the Olympic cake.

My turn in the final approached.

There are two famous quotes by Herb Brooks, head coach of the 1980 U.S. Men's Olympic hockey team, that captured this moment perfectly:

"Great moments are born from great opportunities."

This was my opportunity and it was a gift. I didn't want to let this chance go to waste and I wanted to leave everything I had on the competition floor without regrets. I knew my plan was unorthodox, but I also knew that I couldn't have lived with myself if I didn't try. Completing this routine at the Olympics would be nearly impossible, it's true. But that leads me to the second Herb Brooks quote that I'd had bouncing around in my head all week.

In his pre-game speech to his team, Brooks knew the chances of Team USA beating the Soviet Union at the Olympics were slim, but he didn't care about the odds. He told the men:

"If we played them ten times, they might win nine. But not this game, not tonight."

This was my moment. I had failed thousands of times in training, and hundreds of times in competition – but not this time, not tonight.

I raised my hand, fully committed. I decided to go for it, and I didn't care what happened.

When I jumped up on the bar, I told myself, "Go as aggressively as you possibly can. Do not hold back, do not think, do not be tentative. Just go - whatever happens, happens."

I got up on the bar and I did exactly what I told myself to do. I went into attack mode. My adrenaline was pumping from the start, and it helped to know that Igor Cassina, the current Olympic gold medalist, was watching me and my every move. He was just one more person to prove something to.

I wound up for my first release element, the Cassina, and I nailed it. I released the bar at full speed at the perfect time, flew through the air, performed one laid-out flip with a full twist, and I snagged the bar. After the first element, I continued to pick up speed as I circled around the bar. I sped up for the laid-out Kovacs and caught that one too.

Then I did the full twisting Kovacs, and for the final time, my hands found the bar.

I had successfully completed the most difficult elements I had ever packed into one routine, and adrenaline was raging through my veins. All I had left to do was my dismount, which just so happened to be the most difficult dismount being performed in the competition. At the end of a routine of this magnitude, while winding up for a dismount as complex as the one I was about to attempt, I should've been exhausted and barely able to keep my hands wrapped around the bar. But not this time. On this particular day, as I approached my final skill, I felt no exhaustion – only power. I continued through my last few skills, wound up for the triple twisting, double layout dismount, and – BOOM – landed on my feet! I took a small step forward when I landed, but for the second time in my career I received a standing ovation from the crowd.

The fans rose to their feet with applause as my coach jumped a million feet in the air. I looked at him, and the first thing I said was, "CAN YOU BELIEVE THAT JUST HAPPENED?!"

As the crowd was once again thunderously applauding, my coach and I couldn't stop smiling. I could even hear my teammates in the crowd cheering me on with pride. The Chinese athlete who had already performed before me was forced to wait for my score, and I could see him sitting there silently. His routine scored big, but I could tell that he was having to reckon with the idea that I might've just bumped him out of the gold medal winning spot.

At that point in the competition, Team China had won floor exercise, pommel horse, rings, and parallel bars, and there was no doubt that they wanted to finish the Olympic competition by adding high bar to their list of gold medal winning performances. When the score came up, I posted a 16.175, only .025 behind the Chinese athlete. Had I not taken that small step on the landing, I would have won the gold medal.

As bummed as I was to be so close to gold and not get it, I couldn't help but feel elated about the experience. It was also nice to know that I had once again won the crowd – they were actually upset when I didn't win. They were whistling and booing because they disagreed with my score, and they were Chinese fans! I couldn't believe it, and I'm unbelievably grateful for the respect those fans showed me and my team the entire time we were in China. Chinese fans know their gymnastics, so it was nice to see their recognition of a rival country's unlikely team performance and that of my individual high bar routine.

It's hard to explain the mixture of emotions I felt when I learned I'd placed second. Although I didn't become an Olympic champion, I feel like I became the people's champion in a way ... and that was almost more special. Would I have loved to listen to the US national anthem at the end of the competition with the gold medal around my neck? Absolutely. But that wasn't what I walked away from the competition with. The most incredible part of that experience was being able to look at where I came from, remember all the people who told me it wasn't going to be possible, think about all the times I had fallen over and over again, and know that in the most perfect moment I was able to rise to the occasion.

That's what it was all about. My entire career was about waiting for the right moment to be on top of my game. I hit my peak right when I needed to.

That's what I think every athlete wants to do. We train for decades so that we can be the best at the right moment, and I'm fortunate to have been able to do just that.

Out of all of the competitions I ever participated in – Olympics, nationals, or otherwise – none of them compared to what I experienced at the 2008 Olympic Games.

If I'm being honest, though, even my silver-medal-winning moment didn't compare to earning the bronze medal with my team. When I stood on that medal podium with my teammates next to me, and looked to the left and to the right at Raj, Justin, Alex, Kevin, and Joey, I thought about everything we'd gone through to get there. I thought about the countless hours of training, the way our team had changed, and the emotions we all felt a few nights before on that balcony. To be able to win a medal with those guys, to watch our flag raised up and to know that we'd proven to ourselves and everyone else that we deserved to be there? That was my all-time favorite experience in gymnastics. That moment was golden.

(See what I did there?)

I mentioned earlier that no one believed in us. Even the television network thought so little of our chances that they weren't originally planning on airing the men's gymnastics team final. But since we did so well on our first two events, they cut the coverage over to our competition!

Bob Costas came on the air to say that something was happening with the USA men's gymnastics team, and that we were on fire. He told the audience that they were going to go to the gymnastics arena live and watch what Team USA was doing.

They didn't show my first two events live, but they never took the coverage away from gymnastics once they'd began showing us. Typically they bounce back and forth between a few sports, but they put it on men's gymnastics and kept it there until we were done.

We had turned disbelief and doubt – including our own – into a moment the whole country wanted to follow.

It was truly unforgettable.

Of course, we had no way of knowing the extent of the impact our Olympic performances had made. Once we got home, we realized that it was beyond our craziest expectations.

The Triumphant Return Home

We had no idea what kind of buzz we were stirring up at home until we returned to the USA. Madness ensued from the moment I stepped off the plane and onto American soil. As I was making my way to a connecting flight, people began to bombard me with requests for pictures and autographs as I heard shouts of, "Hey, you're Jonathan Horton, we saw you on TV!" I hadn't really experienced anything like that before. I was by myself, and I didn't have anybody to help me out, and I thought, "WHAT IS HAPPENING?!"

I finally made my connection and flew home to Houston. Haley (not yet my wife) picked me up from the airport so that we could spend some time together before heading back to Oklahoma for school in the fall. As I pulled into my parents' driveway, I was once again unprepared for what was about to happen. Word that I was flying in had gotten out in my hometown neighborhood and by the time I had arrived at 9:00 p.m., there were hundreds of people waiting for me in my parents' front lawn!

Once again – *bananas!* There was even a news crew there to capture the moment. When I pulled up to the house, though, I needed to use the restroom REALLY badly. I couldn't get into the driveway and was telling everyone to get out of the way! After I ran into the house, I came out and signed autographs for two to three hours on the front lawn of my parents' home. I want to formally apologize if I seemed rude during my desperate attempt to get to a bathroom! That was really, really cool and I enjoyed it, but… bananas.

For almost a year, I had to be "that guy" and request a special table in the back of restaurants because fans would interrupt my time with friends or family. I'm not a pretentious guy and I hated to have to do it at the time, but I did want to be able to decompress and enjoy my time with the people I was close to. I just didn't realize the impact that our performance in China had on people at home.

I also had a ton of fan mail that my parents had to help me with. I probably received over 1,000 letters in the mail, and I felt pretty overwhelmed. As much as I hated to do it,

I ended up having to write a generic response to all the fans who had written to me. I just couldn't answer all of it personally, so a standard "thank you" along with a signed photo had to be sufficient.

Obviously, fame is fleeting. I'm recognized in public maybe once or twice a week now, but that time in my life was wild.

The most rewarding part of my experience in Beijing was being able to see the impact I'd had on other people and share my story with them. Looking back, I think that's what inspired me to become a motivational speaker – I remember how it felt when I first heard people say that they could relate to my journey.

Sometimes I wish I could go back for a minute. I think I would soak it in more and enjoy those precious moments with fans. I know there are a lot of people out there who become super famous and get frustrated with that level of fame. Of course there were moments when I didn't want to be bothered just like any normal person. I get it. I can understand how celebs go crazy with the lack of privacy, but for me, I remember too clearly what it was like to be in the fan's shoes.

When I was a kid, I got to meet Blaine Wilson and John Roethlisberger. These guys were my two greatest heroes and mentors in the sport of gymnastics! Now, I'm lucky enough to call them close friends, but back then, I'd run up to them like a crazy person. I wanted nothing more than a picture and an autograph from Blaine and John. I remember the time they were performing at the John Hancock Tour of Champions after the 1996 Olympics. When the tour came to Houston, I stuck my hand over the side rail just as Blaine and John ran by. They each gave me a high-five, and in that moment, I was mesmerized.

When I reflect on those moments, I remember the impact they had on me. I've been blessed to be able to do the things I've done in this sport, and my story is special to some people. There are people that feel about me the way I used to feel about my heroes – I know that I can't take that for granted and I try to approach each of those special moments with appreciation and humility.

Preparing for the Next Olympic Cycle

After seeing my gymnastics heroes perform in the 1996 post-Olympic tour, I was looking forward to being part of that myself after the 2008 Olympics.

My teammates and I traveled around the country for three months doing shows and hanging out with kids and fans. I felt like a rock star for those three months! We did shows in 38 cities and it was an absolute blast. I felt like the tour was a bonus level after an incredibly rewarding game. I love to entertain, so being in front of people putting on a show, dancing, and making people laugh was exhilarating. To be clear, I'm a terrible dancer. I did my best, ok? I loved that people got to see the other, zanier side of the Olympians.

After the tour, I came home and finished up my senior year in college. Think about how crazy this schedule was:

I was in Beijing for the Olympic Games for a month, then performed for three months on tour, then came home and hopped back into my final year of college. Most college students plan their last semester to be their easiest one. Mine was, without a doubt, the most difficult semester of my life. Because of World Championships, the Olympic Games, and all the competitions and events I had done while I was in college, I missed several semesters of school. As a result, I had to make up for it during my last year. In my last semester, I took on 19 credit hours.

For a guy who had never taken more than 12 hours in one semester, it was brutal! All my teammates and other classmates experienced some "senioritis" and had it fairly easy during their final months of college. Not me. This was the price and I was more than willing to pay it.

I graduated. Despite my one-year head start, Haley and I actually graduated together. She received a science degree and I got my degree in Business Management. As soon as we graduated, we married in June of 2009.

At this point, there was a big decision to be made. My wife was going to attend medical school and had been accepted to a few of her top selections. The choice was ultimately between Oklahoma and Houston. If we stayed in Oklahoma, Haley could attend OU Med and I could keep training with the college team and Mark Williams, who had coached me through my collegiate career and first Olympics. If we moved to Houston, Haley would attend medical school at the program that, in our opinion, was a better fit for her (with in-state tuition). Honestly? I wasn't sure if I wanted to move back to Houston to train for the next four years. I had been really happy at Oklahoma with Mark and my teammates. But I knew that Tom Meadows, who coached me prior to college, was a phenomenal coach and would be there for me in Houston. I knew I was going to make another run at the Olympics and I'd always dreamed of taking Tom to the Games.

So we had to choose between two fantastic options. We decided to move to Houston! Leaving Oklahoma was really difficult, but Tom and I were pumped to be back together again.

Haley and I moved into a small house in a suburb south of Houston. I drove 45 minutes every day across town to the gym, while Haley had a 15-minute drive to medical school. Our newlywed lives consisted of studying all day for Haley and training all day for me. It was not an easy transition, and it was about to get even harder. Although I made money on the tour and had saved money from the Games, I needed to get a job. I didn't have any sponsors at the time and our finances became tight really fast. Thankfully, Aaron Basham, owner of Cypress Academy and my former coach, gave me the job I needed. I'd hit the gym at 9:00 a.m., train until 11:00 or 12:00, take a quick break, and proceed to coach until 9:00 every night.

At the end of the day, I'd come home and see my wife. She'd be exhausted and on her way to bed. I knew had to go to sleep, too, because I had to wake up the next morning at six or seven to eat and get ready for the day. I was gone all day, only to get home, eat, and crash.

Coaching wasn't necessarily something I had a passion for, but I was pretty good at it and it paid the bills. I loved being able to support Haley, but I knew it was hurting my training.

I quickly reached a place where I was too tired to train. Luckily, I was still on top of my game after Beijing. 2009, after all of that transition, would become my first year to win the U.S. Nationals after placing second three times before.

Quick side note: I believe I have more second place Men's National Championship finishes than anyone else. I finished behind a different guy every time!

Finally, in 2009, I broke through to win my first National title. I then made it to the World Championships and proceeded to have an absolutely pathetic performance. It was bad – really bad. I had such high expectations for myself coming off the 2008 Olympics and 2009 Nationals, but I think my body just shut down. Because of the schedule I was trying to keep, I was exhausted.

I was prepared for the competition, but nothing went according to plan. I was falling on everything from the very beginning. I fell on floor, pommel horse, and high bar. We were even in London, where the 2012 Olympics would be in three years! I was one of the guys everyone was expecting to take home some medals, but I fell apart and finished close to the back of the pack. I did make the high bar final again, though. I was the reigning silver medalist on high bar and I tried that difficult routine again … but had a much different outcome. I landed on my face. I missed my releases. I didn't land my dismount.

It was embarrassing to say the least.

This was just pretty typical for my life, I guess. There seemed to be no consistency.

After that World Championships, Haley and I made the decision that I would stop coaching. I didn't really know how we were going to make it work financially, but my brief coaching career ended and I was able to concentrate on training full time. I started doing two-a-day workouts again and stayed 100% focused on my goal to go to the 2012 Olympics.

I wanted to win that gold. I was so close in 2008. My dream of standing on top of the medal podium with my team continued to be a daily vision that I couldn't escape.

By God's grace, I signed on with a sports agent in 2009 after I stopped coaching. A wonderful woman named Janey Miller from a sports agency called Octagon came into my life and changed everything for Haley and me. She was such a blessing. Janey was able to lock down several sponsors for the big upcoming years. I signed on with sponsors like BP, BMW, Ralph Lauren, Deloitte, and TD Ameritrade. I'd never been so thankful to be able to simply focus on gymnastics.

Now that the financial burden had been lifted from my shoulders, my ability to train and perform was changed in a hugely positive way. In 2010, I won my second consecutive U.S. National title and made the World Championship team again. As history has proven, when I blow it one year I'm usually on fire the next. I drop the ball and bomb, then I follow that up with something special. In 2010, for the first time ever, I won an all-around bronze medal at the World Championships and became only the fourth male gymnast from the United States to win an all-around medal at that competition.

Our team finished fourth that year and that was a tough pill to swallow. But still, it felt good to get my first world medal under my belt

By winning a World all-around medal, I had the opportunity to stand on the podium with the best male gymnast to have ever graced this planet. Japanese gymnast Kohei Uchimura, who won basically everything from 2009 to 2016, was that guy. Kohei won the 2012 Olympics, the 2016 Olympics, and all the World Championships in between. It had never been done – no one had ever gotten close. He was the athlete that everybody in the world looked up to. To be able to stand on that podium with the greatest gymnast ever was a bit surreal. A good friend of mine from Germany, Philip Boy, placed second. He and I had a pretty epic back and forth battle for the silver and bronze medals. It could have gone either way.

That bronze was a phenomenal thing, but it only barely overshadowed my second favorite prize - an Aston Martin. When I got home, I had to pay a little visit to Aaron Basham. We'd had a very interesting discussion before I went to Worlds. Aaron happened to own an Aston Martin DB9, and I always loved that car. Before I left, I told him, "Hey, Aaron, only three male U.S. gymnasts have ever medaled in the all-around at a World Championships. If I win a medal, you've got to give me the Aston Martin for a weekend." He said, "You know what? Deal."

When I came home, bronze medal in hand, Aaron very happily handed me the car keys. I decided to take Haley out on a little weekend vacation in that gorgeous ride. I'm a BIG car person. I love anything with wheels and a motor, including motorcycles. Having the opportunity to take a car like that for a weekend put a child-like smile on my face. I didn't race in the Aston ... more than once.

That year, 2010, I was better as a gymnast than I was at any other point in my career. I felt strong and powerful. Even though 2008 was the best I'd ever performed, I believe that 2010 and 2011 were the peak years of my gymnastic ability. I was the strongest I'd ever been on rings, the most powerful I'd ever been on floor, and the quickest and sharpest I'd ever been on high bar and parallel bars. So when people ask me, "When do male gymnasts peak?" I can only answer based on my own experience – somewhere between 24 and 25.

There's a First Time for Everything

After that fourth-place finish at the World Championships in 2010, Team USA gained even more positive momentum. By 2011, we had become one of the big powerhouse teams in the world. Our team was fortunate to have a new group of young guns coming up from the junior ranks who started showing some phenomenal promise on the international stage. Soon-to-be superstars like Danell Leyva, John Orozco, Sam Mikulak, and Jake Dalton all came out of the woodwork and blew up the gymnastics scene. They were all under 20 years old, and as the reigning national all-around champion I was the leader of the team ... and an old man.

During the 2011 U.S. Nationals, I finished second. This was after finishing in second place three times before finally earning the title of National Champion in 2009 and 2010. Now I was in second place again, beaten by up-and-coming rock star Danell Leyva, who was six years my junior.

The World Championships that year was in Tokyo, Japan. I was so strong and so good that year, and I felt like I was exactly where I needed to be. For the first time since the Olympics, we won a medal as a team. We were back on the podium and earned a team bronze. China won, Japan placed second, and we were very close to beating Japan on their home turf. Team USA was on the rise!

Here's how it all went down.

We started out on pommel horse. Personally, I don't do pommel horse at major international events (for obvious and comical reasons), but as a whole our team was fantastic on horse. Team USA hadn't been a solid pommel horse team in many years, but our young rookies had finally taken the pommel problem off of the table. We were one of the best, if not the best team in the world on that event for the first time in decades. The world took notice – we had finally filled in the gap on our weakest event and made it one of our strongest.

Then we went to rings, which was my event. I performed my routine the best I could, and it was one of the highest-scoring routines in the world at the time.

After rings was over we went to vault and that's where things went a little south for me. I had one of the biggest vaults in the competition, but it was fairly new and wasn't as consistent as I wanted it to be. Because it was a new vault, I hadn't competed it more than a couple of times, and this would be my first international meet since learning it. My vault was a forward entry vault known as a Drăgulescu. After I would strike the vault, I needed to launch off, do a double front with a half turn and land on my feet.

During the fourth rotation of the team finals, I took off down the runway to attempt my new vault. After the run and jump, I totally misplaced my hands on the vault, didn't get a good push, and crashed hard on the way down. I landed low with my hands on the ground, and I didn't know it at the time, but I broke my foot and completely tore a major ligament upon impact.

Up until now, I had been a rock for the team health-wise. I'd never been injured at all! I had been a bullet-proof athlete … until now.

After hitting the floor, I actually stood up and walked off. I knew my foot was injured, but I think the adrenaline from the moment gave me the ability to walk away even though I was in a lot of pain. My entire team tried to encourage me. "Hey man, no biggie. It's not the end of the world, we're still in a really good position to win a medal," they'd said. My teammates really picked me up, but I knew we had three events to go and I wasn't sure what to do about my foot.

We still had to compete on parallel bars, high bar, and floor. I wasn't scheduled to compete on floor – what a blessing! The floor exercise was traditionally one of my better events and I'd anchored the team on that event in the past, but the new crew was better than I was. After the lineup announcement, I'd been frustrated over not earning a position on the floor team, but in hindsight, I'm really thankful that those guys were so good and able to cover for me after my injury. That said, I *was* one of the anchors on parallel bars and high bar. I remember warming up parallel bars and high bar thinking, "Oh my gosh, my foot is killing me, and I don't know if I can land my dismounts."

As much as I was thinking about the pain I was in, I knew the guys needed me to help them finish what we started.

I felt my foot swelling and I tried to wrap it up really tightly, but it didn't do much to subdue the pain.

I wanted as much time as possible to rest and assess my foot situation, but my turn to compete approached rapidly. I don't know if it was the injury, or if it was the adrenaline, but I ended up doing the best parallel bar routine of my life. I somehow managed to effortlessly breeze through the routine and finish with a perfectly stuck dismount. After I landed, I thought, "Thank you, Lord. I don't know how I did that but thank you!" My foot was throbbing with more pain by the minute.

Then I walked over to high bar, which would be my final performance for the day. Typically, a gymnast stands underneath the bar as his coach assists him in jumping to the 10-foot-high apparatus. As he lifted me up to the bar, I thought about how strong Tom must've been at the time – I couldn't jump at all. I began my routine and with every element I completed, I could feel the blood rushing to my foot. The pressure was nearly unbearable. Once again, by the grace of God, I nailed my routine with zero mistakes. To this day, I can close my eyes and relive what it was like to fly through the air on that particular dismount. I was 12 feet up in the air – about to impact the floor with my feet – thinking, "This is going to suck." Somehow, I was able to stick my landing again. Praise to God alone.

After high bar was finished, my three incredible teammates rounded out the competition with beautiful floor routines, and we were fortunate enough to stand on the medal podium with bronze medals around our necks. Later on in the day, I realized that if I had not done those two routines we wouldn't have won a medal. I was filled with complete gratitude that my body had held up. But for now, with all of that adrenaline gone, I was in some serious pain.

I typically look for the bright side in every situation, and I even found one with this injury. As I mentioned before, World and Olympic competition isn't just about what the team can do, but there is also an all-around competition and individual event finals. To qualify for the all-around or individual event finals, there is a (very controversial) rule called the "Two Per" rule. Basically, it states that only two athletes per country can qualify into an event final or all-around final regardless of how many of the country's athletes are in top qualifying positions. John Orozco and Danell Leyva had beaten me in the all-around during the preliminary competition, and would have the opportunity to compete in the all-around final. So even though I was right on their heels sitting in fourth place after prelims and well within the qualification placement, I wouldn't be able to compete in the final because two guys from my own country had finished ahead of me. I wasn't going to get to defend my 2010 all-around bronze medal. That was a tough pill to swallow! We had a great team of all-around athletes that year and any one of us could have won a medal. But fortunately, this was an easier reality for me to accept after my injury. I couldn't have competed even if I had qualified. I still believe I could've been a two-time world all-around medalist, but that wasn't meant to be my story.

I was completely exhausted and slept hard the night after the team competition. After the mental and physical effort we all put into an event like Worlds, most of us sleep like babies the night it's all over. But I woke up in the middle of the night, and it's impossible to forget the moment when I stood up to go to the bathroom. Steven Legendre, my teammate who roomed with me, was there when I collapsed to the ground and yelled in agony. Steve got up and said, "Dude, what's wrong!?" I said, "Man, I can't walk!"

I looked at my foot and it was dark black and blue. I ended up having to do a combination of crawling and hopping to the bathroom. I didn't see any color in my foot before I went to sleep, but when I tried to get up in the middle of the night, I couldn't put any weight on it. In the morning our athletic trainer had to bring me crutches. I was hobbling around on my crutches and all of the other competitors were wondering what had happened. "What happened to Jonathan Horton? Didn't we see him finish the meet?" they'd said. I had to tell everyone how I'd hurt my foot on vault. I didn't know the extent of the injury yet, but I knew it was bad.

And, plot twist, my world championship competition wasn't over. I had qualified for ring finals during prelims, which meant I was supposed to compete in a few days. Qualifying to finals on rings had always been a big goal of mine.

I hated training rings because it hurt my shoulders, but I loved to compete it because it was an opportunity to show off my strength. I hoped that one day I would be good enough to be one of the best in the world on rings. Finally, in 2011, I finished in the top eight during prelims and advanced on to finals.

I remember having a conversation with my coaches when one of them said, "Hey, do you realize that in a couple days, you're supposed to compete on rings to try to win a medal?" I wondered how I would do it with this foot. It seemed badly broken at best. The doctors looked at my injured foot and they said that without an x-ray or MRI they couldn't tell exactly what was wrong. It could be broken bones, it could be torn ligaments, or it could just be a badly sprained joint. They didn't know. One of the team physicians looked at me and said, "It's your call, Jon. Do you want to go do a ring routine in ring finals?" I told him I was going for it. I didn't know if I would ever have the opportunity to do this again. If I had to land on this foot, I'd do it. How much worse could it get?

When I got to the ring final, I wrapped my foot so heavily that it might as well have been in a cast. All of the other athletes were saying things like, "Hey, we just saw you on crutches. What are you doing?" I told them I was competing. They all looked at me with the same puzzled look.

Like He had so many times throughout my career, God protected me that day. Maybe He just wanted me to know that I was tough enough to do it. Regardless, I got halfway through the routine and I had never felt so strong. I had a ton of adrenaline and did one of the best strength sequences I've ever performed.

But when I got to one of my last handstands –this never happens – I fell out of my handstand. I stayed on the rings and finished the routine, but I wasn't able to get enough momentum for my normal dismount because of the handstand mistake. I was forced to do an easier dismount. Because of that error, I was able to land my dismount in a way that protected my foot from further injury. See God's hand in that? I got to have the opportunity to compete and fulfill a dream of mine, but not put myself at risk of a more devastating injury.

I finished in seventh place on rings. It wasn't the finish I wanted, but it was still cool to be one of the top gymnasts in the world on the event.

After returning home, I immediately got an MRI to see what was going on in my foot. It showed that I had badly broken two bones and torn a major ligament. I was diagnosed with a LisFranc injury, and it's actually pretty rare.

When I saw my doctor, she said, "I want you to know that for most people, it takes over a year to come back from an injury this bad." With the the 2012 Olympics coming up the following year, this was serious news.

In typical Jonathan Horton fashion, I immediately determined that what she said would not be true for me. I didn't have a year to get ready for the Olympics. In fact, the Olympic Games were only ten months away. I said, "No, that's not an option. I'm going to be on that 2012 Olympic team, so I need this foot to heal fast. Whatever you have to do. Whatever rules you have to break, I need you to fix my foot. I'm coming back from this." I can still see the look on my surgeon's face when she said, "Jon, I don't know if that's possible."

But a few days later, I had the surgery. My doctor was phenomenal. She did a ton of research, consulted with other physicians and surgeons, and came up with a plan to get me back as soon as possible. What were our options? Well… we experimented.

Instead of doing the standard fix, she inserted the screws into my foot in a unique way. She never put me in a cast like standard procedure would call for, in the hopes that we could avoid as much stiffness and atrophy as possible. She let my foot hang free, and we went through an insanely tedious process of recovery. Doc was extremely disciplined with what

I was allowed to do (and not do). I'll never forget when she looked at me and said, "Jon, you want to come back right?"

I told her, "of course".

"Great, do exactly what I say and don't do anything stupid. You could easily ruin this surgery. If you do that, you're absolutely not going to compete again this year." Point well taken, Doc.

All told, I think I was in a boot and on crutches for eight weeks, and I was not allowed to put any weight on my foot for that entire time. It drove me bonkers. But during those eight weeks, I did still manage to train. I don't want to lie in my own autobiography, so I'll say that I followed the rules MOST of the time. I did everything I possibly could with my upper body to stay in shape and get stronger. I was able to almost fully train on parallel bars, high bar, and pommel horse. I even created a special pad to protect my foot so that I wouldn't hit it, and I never stopped training. I refused to slow down.

There is no doubt in my mind that doing what I was doing was dangerous. At any moment, I could have made a mistake, landed on my foot, and had to go back into surgery. But I just believed in it. I had a lot of faith in my ability to be smart and make good decisions, even though some people told me I was being reckless.

Okay, everyone told me I was being reckless.

I treated my physical therapy like my seventh gymnastics event, and began to return at record pace. I'd never had to do physical therapy before, but I told myself, "Jon, do more than anybody else. Come back faster than anyone has ever seen. Defy every single statistic. Beat the odds and destroy the doubt that people have about your return." Six months after surgery… there wasn't a single skill or routine I couldn't do.

Now, my foot did feel like it was on fire. Every single time I did a floor routine, I had to heavily wrap it. My surgeon assured me that it was completely healed, but we knew that the pain was just going to be part of it. To me, that wasn't a problem. I was fine with being in pain, but I was not missing out on the Olympic Games. I had to make some adjustments and try some new things in my floor routine, and I wasn't able to get my upgraded vault back, but I was still able to do what I needed.

The strength and power in my legs never quite came back– my vault and floor routine were really not the same after that injury. But by faith in myself and trust in God's plan, I was able to recover and qualify for the Olympic team in 2012. Not only that, but another dream came true when I was elected to be the captain for Team USA. Mission accomplished.

The Comeback

Let me start by saying this:

The 2012 Olympic team, consisting of Jake Dalton, Danell Leyva, Sam Mikulak, John Orozco, and myself, was ridiculous – ridiculously good. Our new guys were absolute rock stars and rose quickly to an incredible level of elite maturity. Because of my injury, I had become a specialist. This meant that I would focus on rings and high bar in London. While I would only be competing on those events in team finals, our team really needed me on those two. I was completely comfortable being the leader of that team with a less active presence in the lineup. I certainly had less stress about my personal performances going from five events to two, but I felt a ton of responsibility when it came to keeping the team excited, calm, cohesive, and every other thing we needed to be great. I felt a huge responsibility to help shape and mold those intangible characteristice of our team.

In the preliminary round of team competition at the 2012 Olympic Games, Team USA destroyed the rest of the field. It wasn't even close! We were in first place by over two and a half points; this was very unusual at the Olympic Games. We were on our way to becoming Olympic champions. We had completed the first step and felt pretty confident in the days to come. We had proven to ourselves, and to the rest of the world, that we had the physical ability to be the best. Our collective performance abilities were peaking at exactly the right moment and we were expecting ourselves to go into the finals and earn a team gold. I believed my dream was going to come true. I was finally going to get to stand on the podium, watch Old Glory go up, and listen to the Star Spangled Banner with a gold medal around my neck. No question about it.

As great as we were, I knew there was something about this team that was different from the Team USA of 2008. To this day, I can't really put my finger on what it was. Maybe it was because we didn't really have the cohesiveness and brotherhood the challenges from Beijing produced. Maybe it was because the 2012 team was so young. Maybe it was Team USA's newfound recognition as a "top dog" from Worlds in 2011 and prelims in 2012 that was tough to handle. Or maybe it was a combination of a few of these things and a few I haven't come up with yet.

Regardless, in the finals round, Team USA fell apart. Our performance was disastrous. Even the members of the team who didn't contribute falls walked away knowing that there were major things we could've done differently. We were all shocked. We were disappointed. We were embarrassed.

The pressure at the Olympic Games is unbelievable – I know it very well. But in the near-decade since that team final competition in 2012 I've come to believe that our team (myself included) was too focused on the end result. Instead of being focused on the moment, on doing one routine or one skill at a time, we were all looking ahead. We were thinking about what it was going to be like to be Olympic champions. We were letting our minds wander toward the status and experiences we would gain from the title. It was way too much pressure for a team as new as ours – we simply couldn't handle it. I don't think anyone could've handled it.

The team final was a disaster – fifth place. Not only did we miss winning a gold medal, but we failed to make it up on the podium at all.

I think my team had to go through the same learning process I went through earlier in my career. If you think about other sports such as football or basketball, often times the young talented team doesn't go all the way to the championship because they lose to a more experienced team, even if that team isn't as physically capable. I think the New England Patriots are a great example. Some would argue that most of the recent post season or Super Bowl wins for New England have had more to do with the team's experience under pressure and less to do with being an outright better football team. The same is true in gymnastics. Athletes have to "pay their dues," so to speak, to earn their moment. This takes time.

As I think about the significant challenges and disappointments I experienced in the sport early on in my career, I feel very fortunate to have had them. I definitely didn't enjoy those times but they helped shape me into the competitor I was in the end. This young team, however, had come out of the gates swinging! They had each experienced massive success as national champions and world medalists, but their time for this big, Olympic moment wasn't quite right yet. They were on the brink of becoming Olympic champions at their very first Olympics. Perhaps they were thinking exactly the way I did at my first World Championships: "Winning is a sure thing, let's go get it!" And with a preliminary team competition like the one we had, who could blame them?

But it didn't happen for me at Worlds, and it hadn't happened for them now.

The 2012 Olympic Games was a learning experience for all of us; it just happened to come at the worst possible time. I would never hold a performance against any athlete (I've had my fair share of blunders, remember?), and I believe that every gymnast needs to go through experiences like that one. But man, it hurt. A LOT.

As fortunate as I was and as grateful as I felt to be a two-time Olympian, I've had to process through the bitter taste that Games left in my mouth. I hate that I felt that way, and I still can't quite get it all into the right words. I got to compete at the Olympics! To wear the red, white, and blue with USA across my chest, twice!

But twice, I was unbelievably close to becoming an Olympic champion and it never happened. In that moment, I feel like I did everything I could to embrace and encourage my team. To tell them that everything would be okay. That we would all move on and be stronger for having had the experience. In retrospect, I think I buried a lot of my own hurt in the process.

To be clear, I've never felt any bitterness toward an individual team member. I care for all of them deeply. But that experience was an extraordinarily painful one, and it's taken quite a while to process through and heal from. If I'm being honest, I've always struggled with how to handle feeling like I let people down.

BLAH.

But, while we were in London, I had to set those feelings aside. I'd qualified for the high bar finals again and would be competing in just a few days. Unfortunately, though I did a great routine, even that performance had lost its magic. I completed my routine successfully and finished in sixth place.

I competed in the Olympic Games for a second time, didn't make any mistakes in the medal rounds, and walked away with nothing. Ouch.

We all live and we learn. There are many beautiful things to take away from that experience. I get to call myself a two-time Olympian. I'm honored to have been the captain of that team. My family got to go with me and experience the pure joy of the Olympic dream. I was finally able to support my wife as a professional athlete. But the experience as a whole was a hard one.

London also revealed another major issue. My right shoulder had been hurting leading up to the Olympics. I was once again one of the best gymnasts in the world on rings, but when I landed my dismount in team finals I felt like I was going to puke because of the pain in my shoulder. I told my coach, "If I had to do one more routine right now, I couldn't do it." I barely missed making the ring finals, and my coach said, "Well, let's count it as a blessing that you didn't make it."

I felt like my shoulder was falling apart from the inside.

After the Olympics, we went on another post-Olympic tour. This time we did 40 cities over three months, and again it was a blast. For me, it was something of a healing experience. It was the first moment that I was able to think, "Okay, I know the Olympics didn't go well, but it feels good to be back out performing and putting smiles on people's faces." The negative? I was in absolute agony every single time I performed – my shoulder was killing me. After tour, my doctor initially said, "Yeah, I think you probably have some tearing in your rotator cuff and maybe your labrum, but we won't know until we get an MRI." I got the MRI, and he said, "Jon, I've never seen a shoulder that is this badly shredded stay as functional as yours. I don't know how you competed on this thing."

I had gone from being the guy who never got injured to having back to back major surgeries. I knew I wasn't done with gymnastics, though. I knew I wanted to do more with the sport, but the upcoming surgery and year-long recovery tested my desire more than anything else ever had.

This recovery would be different from the first one. For the first time, I experienced feeling "blue" about life in general. I was in more pain than I'd ever felt in my life. While other guys were continuing to improve, I quickly became the old "has been," the "used to be," the "not any good anymore" gymnast. But I've never listened to them before, so why start now? I knew I'd be back.

The Recovery: Would I Ever Do Gymnastics Again?

The surgery was supposed to last two hours – it ended up being five. My surgeon had to repair basically everything. I had a 90% tear of the supraspinatus and sub-scapularis muscles. I had a full labral tear and a partial bicep tear. My acromion bone had warped because of the force I'd put on my shoulder joint over so many years – that bone had to be shaved down and reshaped.

My doctor was honest with me. He said, "Look Jon, this is a potential career-ender. This could be the end of gymnastics for you, and I can't guarantee that you'll ever get back to full strength. If you do, it'll take at least a year. And it'll take closer to two years for you to be without pain."

I've always been a "glass half full" kind of guy. It's never half empty. I remember looking at my doctor and saying, "Okay, you're telling me it could be a career-ender, but if I do everything right, I could continue." After a long pause, he said "It's possible."

I said to my doctor, "Okay, you say it'll take a year. I say six months."

I've been blessed to have some incredible physicians on my team throughout my journey, and my experience with this injury was no different. Dr. Walter Lowe, the Head Team Physician for the NFL Houston Texans, NCAA University of Houston Cougars, and the NBA Houston Rockets, is a world-renowned orthopedic surgeon and one of my favorite guys to have gotten to work with. He knows his stuff! It would have been very easy to have been deflated by what he told me, but I wasn't deterred. At least Dr. Lowe had a great sense of humor; when I came-to in recovery, he looked at me and said, "Man, I'm glad I had my Wheaties this morning. That was intense!"

Sure, I had to accept that my shoulder was messed up, but I wasn't going to let it hold me back. I knew what my goals were, and I was determined to come back with my full strength and ability.

One of the things I'm passionate about sharing with young athletes is how I deal with injuries – they happen regardless of the sport you're in. I just give the gymnastics analogy because that's what I know best. Every time I've ever gotten hurt, I've taken physical therapy as seriously as any other aspect of my training.

As I mentioned earlier, there are six events in men's gymnastics. I chose to turn physical therapy into the seventh. I made the decision that I would be the greatest physical therapy patient to ever walk this planet. I would do everything my doctor and my physical therapist told me. I would ask them, "How much harder can I push?" I remember my physical therapist asking me, "Okay, how many days do you want to come in every week? Two, three, or four?" I responded with, "How about five?"

I treated my physical therapy like it was gymnastics and no different. My doctor was blown away by how quickly my range of motion returned. And in a matter of six months – just like I promised – I was doing gymnastics again. I certainly wasn't at full strength, but I was headed in the right direction. After about a year, I was back to 100%! I was doing everything I had been doing at the 2012 Olympics and more.

I also used that time as an opportunity to make my legs as strong as possible. I was in the gym every day, trying to get my legs to be as powerful as they could be. If I couldn't use my arms because of the shoulder injury, I was going to maximize the ability of my other two limbs.

I look at rough situations as if there is always something positive to be found. I would pray and ask God every single day, "God, will you show me why this is good? Will you show me why this is part of your plan?" And you know what? It was hard for me, as a man of faith, as a man who tries to put God first in everything I do in my life, because I started questioning, "God, why? Why am I in this situation, and why does this have to be part of the plan?"

Any person of faith might be tempted to wonder, "God, are you even there? Why do you let bad things happen to good people? I've been faithful."

I went through a time when I was blue. I was down, but overall, I kept most of those feelings at bay. I did my best to stay positive, and I got through it. But I was always wondering, "Why? I should be stronger than this. I'm better than this. I've been bulletproof until this point."

But now we're in 2014. My physical therapy had come to an end and I had scratched my way back to where I wanted to be with my routines. I was close to being able to compete again … until my visit to the Olympic Training Center in Colorado.

Throughout my career, I went to the Olympic Training Center about every two or three months for 20 years straight. From the time I was 11 years old, I trained at the OTC and it felt like my second home.

I had many wonderful experiences at the OTC, but my worst moment there happened in 2014. During one of my typical training sessions, I was having a fantastic workout. I had successfully returned from a potentially career-ending injury, and a lot of people were saying, "Wow, man, I can't believe you've come back. You look strong again." It felt good to have my coaches and teammates take notice of the effort I had put in to getting back into competitive shape. I had always known it was possible, but the reality that I had done what I'd set out to do, against so much adversity, was starting to sink in.

It was at that very moment that I had a freak accident on parallel bars on the final day of training at camp. I did a skill called a Suarez, in which you do a backflip with a half turn between the parallel bars, and it went horribly wrong. The skill requires you to catch yourself on your biceps, and I'd probably done thousands in my career. But on this day, I went a little sideways and I caught the bar right in my armpit.

The impact ruptured my left pectoral muscle.

I didn't know what happened at first. I struck the bar, and I jumped off immediately. I was in extreme pain, but I wasn't sure exactly why. I don't know what it feels like to be shot, but I imagine that it would feel something like this injury. It felt like somebody had just taken a gun, put it to my shoulder, and pulled the trigger.

When I jumped off the apparatus, nobody knew what happened. All my teammates and coaches just stood around with weird looks on their faces trying to figure out why I was pacing around the gym like a madman and holding my arm.

My coach looked at me and asked, "What's going on?" I could only say, "Man, something bad just happened." I couldn't even lift my arm up over my head. After talking to the trainers and doctors on campus, they decided that I needed to head to the hospital to determine the extent of the damage. The team did an MRI right away and were stunned. The doctor said, "Wow, full pec rupture. The muscle ripped right off the bone."

Because I'm a silver-lining kind of guy, I focused on the fact that the muscle itself hadn't torn at all. It had disconnected from where it was attached to the bone, but that comes with a better prognosis.

Still, I was unbelievably disappointed. Hadn't I just put so much work into coming back? Hadn't I worked as hard or harder than I ever had in my career to claw my way back to top shape? It felt like it was all for nothing. Square one.

Just like a bad nightmare, I found myself again lying on the operating table fully dependent on the skills of Dr. Lowe. I was expecting another major shoulder surgery, but fortunately, that wasn't necessary. I didn't realize that because of the nature of the injury and repair, the recovery process would be significantly shorter than that of my last injury. When Dr. Lowe told me that I would probably resume full training in three to four months, I felt a giant weight lift off of my shoulders.

My spirits were certainly better after the good news. I remember that right before I went under anesthesia, I said, "Hey Doc, I like big scars. If I'm going to have surgery, and I'm going to go through all this stuff again, I want something to show for it."

He said, "What do you mean?"

I told him, "Cut me big, Doc."

He said, "You want me to give you a bigger scar on your shoulder than I need to?"

I said, "Yeah, man. It's like a tattoo, I want something to show off!"

Doc looked at me like I was a lunatic. I don't want to get him in trouble so I won't go into details, but let's just say that after surgery I gave him a big "thumbs up" for a job well done. Today, I still wish that scar was a little bigger.

Something changed after that second injury. I can't explain why, but after my pec healed, I just couldn't get any stronger. I went through the most miserable 12-18 months of my career after that.

I was eating right, sleeping right, and doing everything I needed to do. Nothing was working. One of my best events was rings where being strong had always been my bread and butter, but I was having a hard time holding my iron crosses and my other strength elements. Suddenly, my best event became another bad dream I wanted to wake up from.

I knew that if I couldn't get my strength back, I had no shot at making another Olympic team. My specialties were high bar and rings, where the U.S. team was weak at the time, so I knew that I would have a place on the 2016 Olympic team if I could simply perform at my normal ability. And if I couldn't find a way to return to 100% on at least those two events? Game over.

The Long Road Back

I did everything I possibly could to get stronger, but it didn't happen for what seemed like an eternity. Finally, for a reason that's still not clear, I broke through and started to see some improvement.

During my time of injury and recovery to full strength, the U.S. National Committee voted for me to stay on the National Team. It's one of the things they have the power to do if they feel an injured athlete is valuable enough to the team. I remember feeling fortunate that they had faith in me – that they trusted me.

At that time, I was the captain of the U.S. team and I feel I had a lot of intangible value for the team. Every organization needs a strong leader, and the sport of gymnastics is no different. It was important for the team to have someone they not only trusted to lead the team, but someone they could also trust to be the voice for the athletes when needed. Every single year, the National Team members voted for the man they wanted to be their captain. Every year that I was selected I was extremely honored, and took the role very seriously. Although I felt a lot of weight on my shoulders, I was always proud to be the team's leader. But as the saying goes, sometimes when it rains, it pours. At my lowest point, while I was fighting tooth and nail to remain a valued contributor to my sport, my team did not vote me back into the captain position.

That was a tough pill to swallow, but of course I understood. This was 2014, and I hadn't done much for Team USA since the 2012 Olympics in London. At this point, several new young superstars were beginning to thrive and take on their own leadership roles within the team. I was really proud when I saw the improvements that were taking place and the way our new athletes were stepping up to the plate, but it certainly didn't make the situation any easier on me. Looking back, I see that this moment was one of many that made the end of my career seem a little more real – like it was a lot closer than I'd realized. I've never spoken about the impact that moment had on me until writing it in this book, because the truth is, it was a lot more painful than I ever wanted to admit. I could now see the end of my career drawing near.

A couple of months later, after getting myself together and continuing to push forward, I was finally able to enter a meet – the 2014 Winter Nationals. This would be my first competition since the pec tear, and it isn't hyperbole to say that it was one of the worst moments of my career. I was horrible – maybe something worse than horrible.

I fell on every single event, and life as a gymnast seemed to be falling apart. I couldn't get myself to rise up and show a single shining moment. Mentally and physically, I was defeated.

After everything I'd gone through – the injury, the training, and finally getting back to a place where I could compete again – the struggle had completely overwhelmed me. For the first time in over 10 years, I did so poorly that I not only lost my position as a spoken leader for Team USA, but I had officially lost my position as a member of the U.S. team.

Honestly? I was at a loss. I didn't know what to do at this point, so I sat down with a couple of my teammates, National Team Coordinator Kevin Mazeika, and my personal coach Tom Meadows to talk things through. I only had one question: "Guys, am I done? Should I just be finished?"

Everybody tried to be encouraging, and I know it would've been hard for them to tell me what I know should've been said:

"Yeah buddy, great career, but it's time to hang it up."

It's not the easy to look someone in the eyes and tell them they should give up on their dreams. I didn't know how to look at myself in the mirror and accept that I had nothing left. Instead, I looked in that mirror, gritted my teeth and told myself, "Jon, you *will not* stop until you see this thing through. You have never quit a single thing you have ever done, and you aren't going to quit now. You're not going to finish your career like this. You're going to get back on the National Team. You're going to show people that you're a fighter, and you're going to give it everything you've got, no matter what, until 2016."

I didn't know if I had a snowball's chance in you-know-what to make it back on the national team, much less a chance to make it to the Olympics again, but I did know one thing – I didn't want to look back on my career and wonder, "What if?"

"What if" is one of my greatest fears in life. I'm generally not a fearful person, but I can't fathom the idea of looking back on anything and wondering what would have happened if I had simply tried. Not trying would have kept me up at night. Leaving the sport before I had exhausted everything I had would have haunted me, and I wasn't about to hang up my grips without knowing that I had nothing left to give.

That competition, the Winter Nationals in Las Vegas in 2014, felt a lot like that competition when I was 11 years old at Future Stars. It also felt a whole lot like the World Championships in 2006 when I bombed. Every time I felt like quitting, my desire to succeed was greater than my desire to quit.

So when 2015 rolled around, I trained ferociously to make a comeback and prove to myself that I still had some gas in the tank. I qualified into my 16th U.S. National championships, and I made a solid statement to my fellow teammates, coaches, fans, and family. Sure, I made a couple mistakes during the competition. But after spending a year off the National Team, I got myself right back on it by finishing seventh overall. Let's be real, I had a pretty successful career from the time I was 18 on, and I never thought a seventh-place finish would be satisfying.

Man, I was wrong. A lot of people approached me after that competition simply to say, "Hey! Welcome back, champ!"

That was all I needed to hear.

End of An Era

I started making some big strides. I felt I was finally getting back to the real Jonathan Horton, after all the years of struggling, hard times, and pushing through. However, during this entire time of recovering and training again, we weren't making any money. My wife and I had several serious conversations about whether I should be finished and get a "real job." We were struggling financially and trying to push through, but it was tight. Plus, we were about to have our second child!

Times were looking up, though, and I began to feel confident in my gymnastics again. I remember telling Haley, "Babe, this is it. I'm back! I'm going to make this Olympic team." She supported me unwaveringly.

In December of 2015, I went to another training camp and experienced the best few days of training I had ever had in my life. For the first time in years, everything seemed to click. During those three days of training in Colorado, I felt strong, I felt confident, and I didn't fall on a single routine.

As is typical, I came home from training camp really exhausted. National team members put a lot into camps, not only physically but mentally as well, and I was pretty beat. My coach wanted me to take the day off, but I said to Tom, "Look, I know I just had a long camp and it was awesome, but I want to go into the gym and just do a little bit. I don't want to get stiff. I know I'm sore, but I'd feel good about a super light work out." At 30 years old, my body loved to get into the groove, only to later show me that it was just kidding. I was able to thwart a lot of the aches and pains by avoiding time off. I was just going to lightly train a little – no big deal.

Tom said, "Okay, cool. I can't make it in to help, but make sure you take it really easy because you need some solid recovery time." So I went to the gym at 8:00 a.m. on a cold, 30-degree Friday morning in December.

I had a key to the gym, so I unlocked the door and worked out by myself. No one else was inside the 80,000 square foot facility. At the very end of my workout I thought, "You know what? I'm going to go to pommel horse. I'll do three to five turns of some basic skills."

While I was on the pommel horse, I was doing my normal thing until suddenly I felt and heard a "POP!" After the pop came a burning sensation. After that, a feeling of a zipper opening from the top of my left shoulder to the bottom. I jumped off of the pommel horse and I simply stood in the gym for a second while I looked around.

My first thought was, "Did something in my shoulder just tear? Did my entire gymnastics career just come to an end on a cold, dark morning by myself... doing pommel horse?" My coach wasn't there, and my teammates weren't there. It was just me.

It was almost poetic.

I just stood there in the middle of the gym unable to lift my arm. That was it.

I grabbed my gym bag and left.

I knew the injury was just as bad as what I had in 2012 with my right shoulder. Without even going to the doctor first, I went home and told Haley, "Something bad just happened at the gym. I'm 100% positive I just ruptured something in my left shoulder."

To her credit, Haley tried to keep me in the game mentally. She said, "No, no, no, no. You're fine. Maybe it's scar tissue from previous smaller injuries. You're okay. There's no way."

With my wife having a medical background, I trusted her. We both knew that there was only a small chance of her being right. She gave me a small inkling of hope. After it initially happened, I wasn't able to really lift my arm, but then it loosened up, and I was able to move it and use it a little bit. Haley tried to reassure me that I may be fine, so I said, "Okay, we'll wait and see."

I actually tried to train for the next month before I went and saw the doctor to confirm the worst-case scenario.

I wanted to believe that it wasn't *really* over yet.

As I trained, I was able to do most of the basic gymnastics elements on every apparatus, but I felt too weak and in too much pain to try anything difficult. I was staying patient and I had hope that maybe my strength would return, but it wasn't happening.

My coach, Tom, tried to comfort me the same way Haley did. He saw me at the gym every single day and kept telling me, "It's scar tissue, man. You broke a piece of scar tissue off. It feels uncomfortable, but you're going to be fine. You're going to come back, and it's eventually going to get better and you're going to be able to start training again. Just rest it, ice it, and stick with the basics."

After doing what I felt I could handle for a while, I made the appointment to see the doc. When I got the MRI, doc approached me with a pretty somber look on his face. "I'm sorry Jon, it's 100% torn, it's all the way through."

I had a completely ruptured rotator cuff, this time on the other shoulder, and would once again need to have a shoulder surgically repaired.

I got the results of the MRI the day before I was supposed to compete at a local competition called the Houston National Invitational. Obviously, I couldn't compete because of my shoulder, but I wanted to watch the meet anyway. Tom was at the competition coaching the rest of his team, and as I walked up to him in the middle of the meet he anxiously asked, "So, man, what'd they say?"

I just stared at him. Before I could even get the words out, I could see him fight back tears as they welled up in his eyes. Tom and I had been together for 20 years. We had gone from a coach/athlete combo where he was the dictator, to partners and friends in my 30's. As I got to the end of my career, we were equals in this Olympic journey together. My injury was also his.

I said, "Man, it's over. I'm done. That's it. The Jonathan Horton era is finished."

He just gave me a big hug, and I proceeded to tell him the prognosis and that there was no way I could come back in time for the Olympics. Our National Team coordinator, Kevin Mazeika, was there as well, and he had the same reaction followed by a simple, "I'm so sorry, Jon."

I'll never forget that final camp before the injury, though. After our training days in Colorado were over, Kevin looked at me and said one of his favorite lines to use when one of his athletes was doing well: "That dog will hunt!" I had a pretty big smile on my face because of what I had accomplished by being able to perform at the highest level once again. Kevin said, "Jon, I can't believe you're back. You look phenomenal. You're ready." After all of that, having to tell him what happened after the MRI wasn't easy.

Since my final injury and my official goodbye to the sport, I've had a handful of people ask me, "What's your legacy? What do you want people to remember you for?"

It's a difficult question to answer. I think I want people to remember me as the guy that refused to quit, even once. I literally pushed forward until my body couldn't take another moment of training. Not one more flip, twist, push-up, or pull-up could be done to advance myself any farther in the sport of gymnastics. I also want to be known as the guy who was dependable when everything was on the line. When it all counted most, I came through for my team.

Of course, I failed plenty of times, struggled mightily from time to time, and I certainly let some important people down on occasion.

But when it really came down to it, whether it was at the Olympic Games or when I was a collegiate gymnast, when my team was on the line, I came through. I want to be remembered as a clutch athlete my team could trust to do the job right. At the Olympic Games in 2008, those guys wanted a medal more than anything, so I came through and I did it for them, not me. In college, when my team needed me most, I want to be remembered as the guy that made every sacrifice I could for my team.

I want to be remembered as the guy who never quit, and as the guy who cared more about the success and well-being of my teammates than anything else. Medals and winning are great, but I'd rather lose with my brothers at my side than win by myself.

Now that I know the end of my story as a gymnast, that the 2012 Olympics was my last hurrah, I sure do wish I could have come home with one more medal for Team USA. But alas, my last Olympic routine was on the high bar in the event finals. That was the last time I'll ever stand on the floor at an Olympic Games, and I'm unbelievably grateful for that moment.

A lot people have asked me if it hurts that we didn't win a team gold medal in 2008. They even phrase it like, "Hey, does it hurt to know you lost the gold medal?" And I always respond with, "We never lost anything. We won bronze." When I reflect back on my career and think about the ups and downs, I realize now that there really were no downs. Every moment was a chance to move forward; every moment was a blessing because I was doing what I loved.

There is only one thing that I would change about my career - only one wish I have that unfortunately won't ever come true.

I wish that I had one last routine.

I never got to experience my last routine, my last moment as a gymnast, the way I wanted to. I would have loved to step up to any apparatus, raise my hand to the judges, and know in my mind, "This is the last one. Everything you've got, Jon. This is it."

I wish that I had a time like U.S. Olympic diver Troy Dumais, four-time Olympian and Olympic medalist who experienced one of the most beautiful moments I have ever witnessed at the 2016 Olympic trials. As Troy approached his final dive, he was out of the running to qualify for his fifth Olympic Games. He told reporters before the event that this would be his final day of diving. As Troy stepped onto the board, his emotions took over, tears filled his eyes, and the crowd stood up and cheered loudly for several long minutes. I don't know what he was thinking to himself, but I'd like to think it was something like, "Troy, this is it. Thank you, USA Diving. This last one is for you."

I wanted that moment.

I had so many amazing experiences, though. I represented my country, I won medals, I was a captain, and many of my dreams came true.

My career didn't finish on my terms, and that's tough for any elite level athlete who has been a part of his or her sport for a long time. It almost makes me want to come back one last time, and I've thought about training just to do a simple routine on one event and have the closure that I really want. I know it's silly, but I'd be lying if I said I didn't think about it.

Rather than thinking about all the experiences I missed out on, I think focusing on all of the blessings I experienced because of this sport is key. I never won a gold medal at the Olympics or won a world championship, or had my final moment, but God blessed me in many incredible ways.

I am thankful for it all – for the relationships that I made, the skills I learned, the life lessons that molded me, the times I got to sit down and talk with Bob Costas and Meredith Vieira on live TV, the time I got to be on the Oprah Winfrey Show, for the feeling of having a medal placed around my neck, of watching my flag go up in the air, and of listening to the anthem play.

I'm also grateful for the times when I got to cry with my teammates, the times when I was on my face, and even the massive failures that forced me to figure out what to do next. I got to do so many things as I travelled around the world. Many of these blessings are ones that most people don't have the opportunity to experience, and I have to remind myself not to take it all for granted.

I pray that every single human being in this world is able to experience a taste of that feeling. I think it's so important for people to look at their lives, to think about the blessings they have, and to think to themselves, "Wow, I hope everyone else gets a moment like this."

⸎

I did have my lows after my gymnastics career ended, though, and it hasn't always been easy to stay positive. When I hurt myself in 2015, I experienced a low that I hadn't felt before and haven't felt since. As much as I try to, it's hard to forget the moments where I found myself sitting on my couch after my sixth surgery, popping pain pills, and drinking Jack Daniels thinking, "What am I going to do now?"

My daughter had just been born, and I couldn't even pick her up. My son wanted to play with me, but I couldn't be there for him, and my wife was holding down the fort while I was sitting on the couch, watching TV, doing absolutely nothing.

In moments like that, when we think we've hit rock bottom, I've learned that we have to search deep into our souls and ask, "What do I have that I need to be thankful for?" instead of "Why me?"

I think every human on the planet has to hit rock bottom and then come out of it to realize how great this life is and how blessed we are. I think a lot about what God has given us, and I want to be an encouragement to people that feel they're at their "rock bottom." Reach out to others, if you can. It never hurts to ask for help. I had to humble myself, and reach out to my wife, to my friends, and to my family, because Lord knows I couldn't have recovered on my own. Do what you can. Claw out of it each and every day.

Ask yourself, "What do I do now?" When you seek with all your heart, you will find the answers you need.

It's cliché to say, but *never* give up!

Even though I had to deal with losing something I loved dearly before I was ready, in time I realized that new and exciting challenges were waiting just around the corner.

The Quest to Find a New Passion

Believe it or not, as much as I hated being injured, and as much as I didn't want my gymnastics career to end the way it did, there was a silver lining to it all.

I got a call from NBC shortly after I got hurt. They said, "Hey, we heard you got hurt. Would you like to come work for us during the Olympic Games?"

I said, "Well yeah… duh. Let's do it."

I was fresh out of my sling, and my injury was healing up at that time. In my wildest dreams, I didn't think I would actually get to do something like this. I had never done any commentary before, but I had always dreamed of being a commentator for the sport just like Tim Dagget and Bart Connor.

NBC has their major headquarters in Stamford, Connecticut. I showed up in Stamford, and I was set to be there for three weeks to do commentary for the live stream of gymnastics competition.

My co-hosts were Courtney Kupets, 2004 Olympic silver medalist, and an amazing play-by-play commentator named Jim Watson. I looked at them and I asked, "You guys have done this before, right?"

Jim replied, "Oh yeah, I've been doing this for 20+ years."

Courtney said, "Oh yeah, I've been doing this for five or six years for the PAC 12 collegiate network."

My simple response was, "Okay, cool... so, what do I do?"

And they asked, "You've never done this before?"

Nope.

I sat down with some producers and we went through a couple classes. I asked, "So what do I do?"

Their best advice: "Just talk about gymnastics." Now that was something I knew I could do.

I thought, "Okay, so I'm not getting any real direction here." Basically, I decided to wing it. I figured that since I'd listened to Tim Daggett, Al Trautwig, Elfie Schlegel, and Nastia Liukin do gymnastics commentary for so many years, I would simply try to do what they do.

I sat down in a little studio with Jim and Courtney, and I was super amped up with adrenaline. I was given an NBC jacket, and the reality of what I was doing began to sink in. Doing this work for NBC was a dream come true for me. I knew I wasn't at the Olympics competing, but this was the next best thing. I still got to participate, even if it was behind the mic.

I sat down and put my headphones on, and immediately noticed how incredible the headphones were. I could hear every little thing!

So as the coverage came on, Jim Watson brought us in and opened with, "Welcome to the 2016 Rio Olympic Games..." Then Courtney said a few things. Then I came on, and my heart was pounding a million miles an hour. I knew I was live, and there were tons of people watching. A lot of people told me later that they tuned in.

It didn't take long to get the jitters out. I started feeling pretty comfortable in my new role, but things got a little crazy about ten minutes into my very first live broadcast. An athlete from France named Samir Ait Said was getting ready to do his vault. I had competed with Samir before, and he's usually a ring specialist, but he's also really good at vault. I said, "Okay, here's Samir. He's going to do this big time vault called a Tsukahara with a double pike back flip."

Samir took off down the vault runway, hit the springboard, and flew over the vault table. As soon as Samir's hands left the vaulting table, I could tell that things were a little off. He went sideways, flipped twice over the vault in the pike position, then struck the mats below.

All we could hear – and remember, these headphones picked up everything – was what sounded to me, Courtney, and Jim like a tree branch snapping in half. Because Samir had pushed himself off of the vault sideways, he flipped on an improper axis and came down wrong on the side of his leg, breaking both bones below his knee. Jim and Courtney, the two commentators with all of the experience, simply froze. I looked over at Courtney, and she looked like she was about to puke. Jim has his mouth wide open staring at the TV screen. I looked at both of them and said, "Uh." Even the cameraman froze and they ended up keeping the camera on Samir as he was lying there with his leg broken.

All of a sudden, Mike, our producer who had spoken to us through our headsets periodically, said, "I'm going to need one of you guys to say something." He usually gave us little tips and pointers about who was coming up next. He was at a loss for words as well, but he reeled us back in at that moment.

I finally said, "Ladies and gentlemen, obviously we're looking at a pretty gruesome injury. I recommend that you look away from the screen if you don't have the stomach for this." And all of a sudden, the cameraman had the presence to pull the camera away from Samir. Jim came back at that moment, but Courtney still looked a little pale.

No offense to Samir, but that moment officially broke the ice for me. I thought, "If I can handle that, I can handle anything." Ever since that moment, I've believed that I can be a successful color commentator.

Aside from Samir's injury, my whole experience turned out perfectly. I really enjoyed being a commentator for the Olympics and it was extremely rewarding to take what I'd been through as an athlete and use it for something new. I felt super comfortable sitting in that chair inside of a little booth doing what I love more than anything – talking about gymnastics. Later on after the Olympics concluded, Sports Illustrated gave us an A rating for our efforts. In fact, they wrote up an article about all of the different commentators for the Olympics, and they gave me, Jim, and Courtney an A. I couldn't have been happier about the solid review.

I ended up getting more work like this from NBC, so I'm assuming they were pleased with the job we did covering the Rio Games. In fact, my most recent commentating experience involved sitting in Denver broadcasting for a World Cup competition in Croatia with none other than my good buddy Jim Watson. We still talk about the gruesome leg injury that kicked off the 2016 Olympics.

It was a cool opportunity for me, and it was certainly unexpected. I'm hoping that one day, God will bless me with the opportunity to be a prime-time commentator for many more exciting gymnastics competitions.

Shoot, maybe I'll get to the Olympics again.

I'll just keep working hard and see what happens. Isn't it amazing how some doors only open when others close?

Ninja Warrior

During the last few years of my gymnastics career, I had also discovered one of America's favorite TV shows, American Ninja Warrior. I would watch it on TV and think to myself, "I can totally do this!" I fell in love with watching the show because of the style of athleticism that it takes to be successful as a "ninja."

When I made it on the show for the first time, I didn't take it very seriously. I was still competing in gymnastics, so I was just having fun and testing the waters – pun intended. I was thinking that with my gymnastics background I would be really good without even trying. That arrogance came back to bite me! I was quickly humbled by the challenges and adversities that Ninja Warrior created. But I thought, "Whatever, I don't care."

Well, that was a big fat lie.

But when I got hurt in 2015 and my gymnastics career came to an end, I started thinking, "What if this is my way to compete? Maybe this is the way to be the athlete Jonathan Horton loves to be."

My very first season of Ninja Warrior was season six in 2013. As I write this book, there have been eleven full seasons of the show. I had seen the original version, called Sasuke, which was filmed in Japan. So naturally I was intrigued when they brought the show here to the U.S.! I kind of assumed that as an elite gymnast, I had all of the skills, agility, and strength that I needed to be successful if I ever tried it out. I was convinced I was going to win this show and make it look easy.

To apply, I had to make a three-minute video about myself and fill out an encyclopedia's worth of paperwork. After it was all done, I received a call back from the producers almost immediately. They told me they would love to have me on the show; however, I tore my pec muscle at the Olympic Training Center right after that call.

Three months after my pec repair surgery, I was supposed to compete on ANW. When I discussed it with my doctor, he said, "Well, it's healed, but you could still injure it again because you're not as strong as you used to be. I don't recommend doing Ninja Warrior, but I'm not going to tell you that you can't."

I decided that I could do it whether I was injured or not, and that it would likely be pretty easy.

That was stupid.

The night before my ANW debut, my wife asked, "Are you sure you want to do this?" I said, "Yeah, I've got it. I'm good."

On the day of the competition, I got up there and my adrenaline was pumping. Suddenly, I found myself about halfway through the course... absolutely exhausted! I jumped up on the fifth obstacle of the night called the ring toss. I'm supposed to be good on things called the rings, right? Well, halfway through the ring toss I took a swan dive into the water. Ironically, I was the seventh best gymnast in the world on rings just two years earlier. Yet here I am, falling off the rings on a TV show called American Ninja Warrior. I was pretty mad, and I couldn't believe I had fallen. I was shocked that I wasn't as good as I had originally imagined, and I was immediately impressed with the competitors that had done really well on the show. I gained an instant respect for what the Ninja Warrior phenomenon was. It's more than a TV show; it truly is a competition for great athletes, and in order to be successful, one needs to take the sport seriously.

The very next year, I applied for the show again and I wasn't accepted. I got a call from the producers during which they very politely told me, "Thanks for sending in your application again. It was really competitive, and we've decided that you aren't going to be one of our competitors this year."

Honesty, I was really surprised. I thought I was going to have a shot at redeeming myself! I felt ready to face the course because I was finally strong again, and had been surgery-free for an entire year.

Luckily, I had another option. The show has a "walk-on" line for the people who aren't given spots to compete. Anyone with a desire to be on the show (and a lot of extra time) can wait in line for five to seven days and camp out overnight at the site where the course is set up. Usually, only 50 people or so are allowed to stand in the line. There are a few fanatics who showed up in different cities a full month ahead of time to try to form that line. Fortunately, the producers won't let it start until a week before filming. Still, standing in line for a week outside just to be on a TV show seems a little insane. I learned quickly that the ninja world has some really die-hard fans who are absolutely obsessed with getting on the show.

In 2014, American Ninja Warrior came to my hometown of Houston, and I remember thinking it would be somewhat reasonable to go stay in the walk-on line since the course was only five miles from my house. Still, I didn't want to stand in a stupid line forever.

Curiosity got ahold of me. I decided to drive past the site of filming just to see what they were all doing. As I was driving by, I saw the line of people that had already been standing there for a few days. I parked and went to go check things out. I figured the line was probably full already, but that I'd go say hello to a few of the competitors I knew. I walked over and I saw everyone camping out in small tents. I asked one of the competitors how long they had been waiting and he told me they had been there for three days already. I said, "Wow, that's crazy! How many people are in line?" They told me that 47 people had initially shown up and that they would take three more.

I was shocked that the line wasn't already full, and I was wondering what the likelihood of number 48, 49, and 50 getting to run on the show were – probably slim to none. I knew that usually 10 to 15 people from the walk-on line would get the chance to run the course, and it felt dumb to even think about camping for several days for a chance at nothing. While I was standing there, one of the producers of the show walked by and said, "Hey, you're Jonathan Horton!" I said, "Hey! Yes, I am."

That particular producer was involved in casting for the show. He said to me, "What are you doing here by the walk-on line?"

I replied, "Oh, I was just checking it out, but I'm not in line. I didn't get accepted this year, and I was just seeing what this walk-on line thing is all about."

He said, "Well, why don't you put your name down as number 48? I can't believe we didn't accept you this year. You're an Olympian, man, let me see what I can do."

Next thing I know, I had put my name on the list, driven home, gotten some stuff, rounded up some food, and found a little tent. The producer came back later and said to me, "Hey, don't leave. I'm going to work some magic." I asked, "Are you serious?" He said, "Yeah, you just have to stay in the line. Man, you're an Olympian. You should be able to run the course."

I told him that I appreciated the help, but I said to him, "I feel bad. I don't want to jump in front of somebody else." He was adamant that I get a shot at the course because he had seen me run the year before, he knew my story, and knew who I was.

So there I was, sleeping outside for the next three days awaiting my chance. Haley thought I was crazy (not the first time), but I did it anyway. After working the magic the producer had promised, I was the sixth competitor to attempt the obstacles that night, and I became the very first person to beat the course in Houston, Texas. Haley and my kids weren't able to be there to see it, but Mom and Dad were there to cheer me on.

It's always interesting to see how God orchestrates these events in my life. Sometimes I have no idea when they are coming! I stepped up to that course after three days outside and plowed through obstacle after obstacle until I made it to the top of the infamous warped wall. The year before, I had fallen. This year, I wasn't accepted onto the show. Then BOOM – I'm on the show, running the course in my hometown, and I'm crushing it. I've done some really cool stuff in my time as an athlete, but making it up that warped wall as the shortest person to ever hit the buzzer ranks pretty highly on the list. The smoke went up, the place went crazy, and I went crazy!

I remember being on one of the obstacles when the crowd recognized who I was. They don't normally announce the names of the athletes to the live audience, but everyone saw the Olympic Rings tattooed on my back and word travelled quickly. The live event feels quite a bit different than what is seen on TV because neither the crowd nor the competitors can hear the commentators, but even without hearing my name, everyone began chanting "USA, USA!" That moment took me back to a little bit of old-school Olympic glory.

What was most special about it, though, was thinking about the struggle I was enduring as a gymnast at the time. Not much was going right in my gymnastics career during that season of life. Suddenly, I was standing at the top of the warped wall feeling like a champion again. I felt like I was on top of a medal podium, receiving praise from fans and feeling like an accomplished athlete.

Of course, after I finished the course on night one and advanced to the city finals, I ran the extended course that second night and fell on the eighth obstacle. I wound up in 16th place – only 15 competitors advanced to the national finals.

That result stung, and I may have finished in the worst position possible, but I realized how cool it was to hit the buzzer on night one. Ninja Warrior was like a drug to me after that season. I'd hit one buzzer, and I wanted to hit more.

There are some things about American Ninja Warrior that a lot of people don't realize that makes this even harder. Most people don't know that ANW is filmed in the middle of the night. Filming begins around 9:00 p.m., when the sun goes down, and stops when the sun rises. Every time I've ever run the course it's been between 1:00 a.m. and 4:00 a.m., which is definitely a big challenge. Ninja competitors basically have to become nocturnal for weeks at a time to be successful on the courses. Several of the really serious competitors will sleep train themselves for months before competing.

It should also be noted that the show producers don't allow competitors to practice the course at all until it's our turn. This was a big change from gymnastics and I needed to get used to it. As a gymnast, I did the same routines over and over again for years. I always knew what to expect and I had control over the performance. I was sure that if I trained really hard and had enough successful routines under my belt, all I'd need to do in competition was step up to the apparatus, turn on the autopilot, and be sure not to let a mental mistake occur. However, with Ninja Warrior, it's different. It's more like, "hey, here's this massive obstacle course you've never done, and we aren't going to let you on it before you compete. Have at it!"

The first time we touch any of the obstacles is what you see on TV. That represents a big challenge for me. I've had to let go of the fact that I don't know what I'm doing and force myself to be aggressive. This mentality can be tough for a lot of elite gymnasts. When we are learning new skills and new routines, it's hard to be really aggressive because we fear injury if something goes awry. As a result, we have to ease our way into attack mode. But we can't really ease our way into anything on Ninja Warrior. We have to be aggressive on every obstacle, from start to finish, or we're going to end up in the water.

That's probably been the toughest transition for me – learning to attack the unknown. I look at some of the younger and more successful Ninja competitors with absolute amazement. They have no idea what's coming at them, but they have tons of success as ninjas because they are fearless. After so many years of Ninja competition, I've come to realize that I have to get out of my gymnastics state of mind, turn into a kid again, go as fast as I can, and have a blast.

All things considered, the community of Ninja competitors and the atmosphere of the sport is fantastic. Ninja sports programs are growing rapidly across the world because of the success of American Ninja Warrior on television. Thousands of standalone obstacle training facilities have been built, new versions of the show have been created, and hundreds of private competitions take place every year. It's such a great world to be a part of.

As the sport has grown, so has my passion for it, and missing out on the national finals led me to train even harder for the 2015 Ninja Warrior competition. By that time, I was in great shape because I was preparing for the Olympics again. Unfortunately, it was then that I was struck with my final shoulder injury. When I missed out on my shot at the

2016 Games, I also missed out on being able to compete in Oklahoma City for Ninja Warrior Season 8. That period was the deepest depth of my rock bottom moment. I wasn't going to get another shot at either of the things I loved and had worked for, and it ate me up inside.

As 2016 rolled around, I was recovering from my shoulder surgery, and reality had set in that I wasn't going to be doing gymnastics anymore. I knew I had a good comeback story to tell, so I made sure to apply for the show. When I did my submission video, I talked about going through my injury, missing out on the Olympics, all of the hardship I experienced, and how I wanted to compete on Ninja Warrior again to prove to myself that I still had some greatness within me as an athlete. I told them how I'd struggled with feeling like I had lost my purpose, which to me was always to perform under pressure and live out life as an elite athlete. Ninja Warrior was the only outlet I knew about that could give me those feelings again.

NBC called right away to tell me they wanted me back on the show.

I ran the city qualifier course in San Antonio, Texas, and by the grace of God, I finished every obstacle. My story was blown up on TV. In fact, they put me in as the last competitor on the show and highlighted the drama about whether or not Olympian Jonathan Horton could come back from so many injuries. The producers told my story emotionally and truthfully; it was really beautifully done.

I made it up that wall and hit the buzzer again, and an iconic moment was born.

When I reached the top of the wall, I turned to the hosts of the show and flexed while I hung there on one arm. Someone in the crowd snapped a shot as I hung there, and it has become my official logo – a simple silhouette of me hanging atop the warped wall. The picture perfectly depicts what my athletic career has been like – hanging onto an impossible dream, sometimes by one arm, but in the end, I have always pulled myself up. At this moment, I had ridden the crazy roller coaster again. I'd had three to four years of struggle and emotional ups and downs, but this moment was pure joy. As I stood on top of that wall, I felt like myself again.

In spite of falling into the cold dark water at some point every year, American Ninja Warrior has been such a joy for me. I think that's one of the reasons it's been a tremendously successful show! It's all about normal people overcoming extraordinary challenges, mentally and physically. Personally, I feel like it's brought me back to life during times when I was down. What can seem like a silly show about jumping and running has given me and so many others a new platform to be ourselves and pursue something great.

I'm a competitor to the core, but I honestly don't care about falling on the obstacles anymore, as it continues to happen every year. In 2017, I had a rough time on Season 10 when I fell on the fourth obstacle. I also made mistakes in Ninja vs. Ninja, which was a team style show. My team was Paul Hamm, April Bennett, and me – all Olympians. Paul is an Olympic gold medalist in gymnastics and April was an Olympic pole vaulter. We were the Olympic Ninja team … I loved the sound of that. We didn't make it too far into the competition, but at least we had a cool team name. And yes, most recently on Season 11 in 2019, I fell on a simple obstacle in the city finals. For the fifth time, I didn't make it to the national finals in Las Vegas.

I've gotten to experience a lot of really cool things with Ninja Warrior, and while I still have never made it to the national finals, or really won anything on the show, I'll continue to pursue it. Ninja is very therapeutic for me. It reminds me of my gymnastics days. In the very beginning, I had zero success. I never won, I wasn't a finalist, and I wasn't a champion, but I stuck around long enough for a glimmer of something great to show up. I may be great as a Ninja one day and I may not, but I know that if I don't keep going, I'll never have the opportunity to find out.

It's been a blessing from God for me to have something new to pursue. In fact, one reason I keep going is because of

Isaac Caldiero. As of this writing, he's the only person who has ever won American Ninja Warrior. In ten seasons, only one guy's ever done it, and he said something on TV one time that really resonated with me: "I always tell myself that I want to go find my impossible and conquer it." When he won the show, he said "I found my impossible and I did it."

That's what I feel like I'm always trying to do in my life. I look for what's impossible and go try to beat it. In gymnastics, it was to make the Olympics, become a medalist, and win a gold medal. I found my impossible and I set out to conquer it. Now I'm doing the same thing with American Ninja Warrior, I'm doing the same thing in my current career as a motivational speaker, and I'm doing the same thing as a father and a husband.

Sometimes it feels impossible to raise kids, but I'm going to conquer it.

Sometimes it feels impossible to be successful in all of the professional endeavors I'm involved in, but I'm going to conquer those as well.

I'll be back for more seasons of American Ninja Warrior, and who knows? Maybe one day I'll become a Ninja champion. Until then, I'll just keep calm and ninja on.

What If?

Sometimes when I reflect back on my career, I'm struck by the knowledge that my results could have been even better than they were. Of course I realize that there aren't many people who will ever win an Olympic medal, but I still know that more could have been done.

What if I hadn't made so many mistakes? What if I'd committed to my nutrition earlier on in my career? What if I hadn't fallen on routines in key moments?

As I mentioned earlier, I finished second place at U.S. Nationals three times before I finally won two in a row, then I finished second again. I think about my heroes in gymnastics like Blaine Wilson who won five national titles, John Roethlisberger, a four-time national champion, and Paul Hamm, a multiple-time national champion and Olympic champion.

I think about each one of those four second-place finishes – I made really dumb mistakes during every competition. It would have been very possible for me to have won a few more, and had I not messed up on silly things, I could've been a six-time national champion with one of the most winningest records in USA history.

But you know what? Maybe not.

Maybe I would've grown complacent with my training. Perhaps that much success would have made me stop working hard, stop driving forward with every ounce of passion that I have. Maybe without the struggle and heartache I wouldn't have been sharpened into the husband and father I am today. Yes, after coming so close so many times, I eventually broke through, but I believe that it was the amount of "almost" success I experienced that helped me become an Olympian, national champion, and world medalist.

Maybe God's preparing me in the same way when it comes to Ninja Warrior, and the rest of my life. Maybe He knew that if I had gotten on the show during Season 1 and blown it out of the water, then I would never have experienced the beautiful moments I've been given since. I've never been a fast learner or quick to succeed in anything I have pursued in my life, and I'm starting to think that it's for the better.

I have always been really thankful that I was able to win that silver medal on high bar, but sometimes it still stings to know how close I came to gold. I lost out on gold by less than a tenth of a point, which even in gymnastics is basically nothing.

But there's something my dad told me one time that was extremely profound.

A couple of years after the Olympics, I was speaking with my father about my silver medal, and he looked at me and said, "You know what? Maybe a gold medal in 2008 wasn't part of your story because God had more in store for you with your gymnastics career. Maybe if you had won gold, you would've never become a two-time Olympian. Maybe you would've let fame and money get into your head. Maybe you would've let your relationship with Haley go downhill. Maybe God knew it wasn't right for you to have all that money, have all that fame, and let the rock star life go to your head."

Since gymnastics is one of the most popular sports in the Olympics, an Olympic gymnast who wins gold will often experience quite a bit of fortune following the performance – we're talking sponsors, commercials, clothing deals, movies, and so on. Even my sports agent at the time reminded me that the financial difference between a gold and silver at the Olympics was usually millions of dollars.

A lot of people believe that my performance in 2008 should have earned a gold medal, but that wasn't my story.

Maybe Dad was right, though. Maybe I was too young and immature to experience that kind of success. Maybe becoming an Olympic champion would have dulled my desire to train hard going forward. Maybe I would have missed a chance to be on the 2012 Olympic team and impact those young guys who were on the team with me. All of that said, I wouldn't trade my experiences for anything. Representing my country a second time was priceless, and all the hard work leading up to that moment helped shape who I am today.

Maybe God has humbled me all these times to prepare me for more athletic greatness in the future, and maybe not. I don't know. But I trust the work He's done (and continues to do) in my heart.

No matter what happens going forward, I am at peace with my past, and I enthusiastically embrace my future. I know I won't be able to compete as an elite athlete like this forever.

Time marches forward.

Through it all, however, I want to impact those around me through gymnastics, American Ninja Warrior, public speaking, and the telling of my story.

No matter what happens, my journey will continue.

The Thing That Always Keeps Me Going

I've only recently discovered my passion to share my story with people. One of my greatest desires is to encourage others, especially other athletes, in whatever way I can. My hope is that when someone needs inspiration or needs someone to lean on, they would reach out. I want my story to bring encouragement to people that have big dreams but may need help or guidance to get where they want to go.

I've said before that I believe everyone has a rock bottom moment at some point in their lives – Olympians, actors, comedians, you name it! Even those people who you thought had it all together. I never want anyone to think their situation is hopeless. It isn't! And it's important for people to know there are others out there who not only feel that they have the ability to help, but who want to!

When I was trying to process through the finality of my last injury and the end of my gymnastics career, and was wondering what would happen next, things got really ugly. Fortunately, I had an amazing wife, an incredible family, and other close friends to pull me out of it. Was it easy? No!

Life is a constant journey of self-discovery, whether it's learning more about the man I will eventually become, how to be a better husband and father, or how to have the greatest possible impact on the world. The journey is all about running the path, jumping over obstacles, figuring out what's next, and figuring out how it needs to be done. The dream is to be free.

Here's the part of my story that some of you may shy away from, but I pray you don't. I'd like to let you in on my secret to freedom and the joy that I experience every day.

I'm not ashamed to speak about my faith in God - it gives me strength. I'm a man of faith, and I know God is going to free me from any kind of stress or any kind of worry. I know that my freedom is 100% from Jesus Christ, who has saved me and all who believe in Him. I know that one day, when this life is over and I'm in Heaven, I'm going to be free of all sadness, anxiety, pain, or wounds from trials here on earth.

My relationship with God plays the greatest role in every decision I make in my life, and my story wouldn't make any sense if I left out such an essential piece of it. That said, I'd like to share how the gospel of Jesus has changed my life for eternity.

As we all know, we live in a broken world, and it doesn't take much searching to see the brokenness all around us. We see depression, alcoholism, addictions of all kinds, and heinous crimes every day on the news, right? God didn't create this world to be broken, but to be perfect and in unity with Him and His glory. From the beginning, though, human beings have turned away from God, believing that our way of doing things is better. People do everything they possibly can to escape their brokenness by clinging to things like money, possessions, and yes, even medals and titles such as "Olympian."

But as we can see, none of the earthly things we cling to can relieve us permanently from our brokenness. As such, God brought us a savior. Hallelujah!

That savior is Jesus Christ. Christ is the Son of God who came to this earth to make the ultimate sacrifice and pay the price for all of our sins. He died a gruesome death on a cross over 2,000 years ago, but friends, the good news is coming! Jesus rose from the dead three days later and appeared to over 500 people. He calls us all to repent and believe, to turn from our sin and trust in Him alone to save us and reconcile us to God. If we will trust solely in Jesus (not our own good deeds or anything else), we are restored and reunited with God, and when this life ends, we will live an eternity in heaven with our Lord and savior Jesus Christ! I have a smile from ear to ear as I write about the blessing of Jesus.

The story of Jesus is simple, it's true, and it saves all who put their trust in Him to save them. If you are ready to believe in Jesus and live your life for him, and you happen to be reading my book right now, tell Him in your own words that you're sorry for your sin against Him, you want to live for Him, and you believe that He died and rose from the dead so that you could be forgiven. And then find a Bible teaching church where you can grow in your faith and learn how to live a life that glorifies Jesus Christ.

Wherever we are in life, there is a better life in Jesus Christ. That's the only reason I've been able to get to where I am. It's why I can look at people and smile as I share my story. I can tell people about the faith I have in myself, and in other people around me, because of the promise I have in Christ. I believe that Jesus died for my sins, and that if I believe in Him, one day **I'm going to live forever in the presence of God in heaven**.

Friends, life is hard. People think it's all sunshine and roses for an Olympian – it's not. The most successful people on the planet struggle, and no one has it all together. Not one. I keep up with motivational people like Grant Cardone, Gary Vaynerchuk, Tony Robbins, and many other inspirational speakers. Even they cannot tell me they don't have days where they struggle with what's next and feel broken just like the rest of us. All the money in the world cannot buy happiness or a life with no stress or anxiety.

I want the world to know – including those of you who are reading this – that you are *not* alone. The best part of all of this? God is with us!

The Journey Continues

As I reflect on my life so far, I understand very clearly how abundantly I have been blessed. Very few people ever get to experience the things that I have. Few in the gymnastics community believed in me when I was a young kid, and for a while, their concerns were justified. The difference that separated me from so many others is that I didn't give up (even when that seemed like the most logical thing to do).

Gymnastics is really hard! The strength, skill set, and mental game required to excel take a long time to develop. Average people give up when things get hard, but champions persevere until they reach their goal.

I could have given up when I took 50th place out of 50 boys at my major competition. But I didn't, and as a result, I am the only guy from that group who won an Olympic medal over a decade later.

Let that sink in for a moment.

At that moment, I was not even close to being selected to train and participate in higher-level national and international competitions. I kept working toward the goal and eventually bounced back.

My career was a long string of ups and downs. But every time I failed, I stepped up at my next opportunity and experienced a moment of victory.

Now that my time as a gymnast is done, I get to channel my competitive fire with American Ninja Warrior, help young athletes grow within their own gymnastic journey, and speak in front of thousands.

Currently, my son is six years old and he's begun taking his first steps into the sport of gymnastics. It's surreal to think about how he is now close to the same age I was when I started. It'll be fun to watch him grow. In fact, he is catching on to things faster than I did at his age! I suppose I have my wife's genetic influence to thank for that. Will his career surpass mine? I guess we'll see. I will never pressure either of my children because this is their journey, not mine. In fact, my daughter seems to have taken an interest in musical theatre over gymnastics, and I look forward to seeing her grow in that, too!

The beautiful part about all of this – through national championships in college, excelling on the world stage and at the Olympics, and competing in American Ninja Warrior – is that I chose to write my own story. I took many leaps of faith. Sometimes I won, and other times I learned. Through it all, I kept going.

I was an ordinary kid who failed his way to his Olympic dream. I wasn't superhuman or any more special than anyone else. I had a burning desire to achieve my dream, and believe that greatness is within you as well.

Achieving success isn't about the moments of glory everyone gets to see, it's about the behind-the-scenes sacrifices no one sees but you and your coaches, day in and day out. I made empowering choices that carried me to my dream, and you can do the same.

I look forward to seeing what unfolds not only for me, but for you as well. Have the courage to pursue excellence and always keep moving forward.

I believe in you!

About the
Author

Jonathan Horton is a motivational speaker, a two-time Olympic medalist, a professional athlete, and a competitor on NBC's American Ninja Warrior. At the Beijing Olympics in 2008, he helped lead the U.S. team to a bronze medal and brought home a silver medal of his own on the high bar. Horton competed for the University of Oklahoma for four years (2005-2008), earning 18 career All-American honors. Six of those honors came with first-place finishes. Horton was a two-time U.S. National All-Around Champion, and he competed in the 2012 Olympics in London, finishing in sixth place on the high bar. Following a shoulder injury, Jonathan retired from the sport and began his career as a motivational speaker and American Ninja Warrior competitor. He currently lives in Houston with his wife, Haley, and their two children.

Acknowledgments

Although the journey I've described has been told from my own perspective, I know I have not been alone for a moment of my life. I would like to thank the people who have provided my phenomenal support system and who made this book possible.

First, I want to thank my family – my mom, dad, and sister. Thank you for believing in me from day one, for never adding any additional pressure to my goals, and for loving me unconditionally. Mom, you told me once that you knew from the moment I was born that I would do great things, and I thank you for your unwavering belief and confidence. I love you all very much.

To all my coaches, thank you for shaping me from the first moment I stepped into a gym. Every one of you has had an incredible impact on me as an athlete and helped make me into the person I am today.

To my closest friends and teammates. Thank you for the amazing experiences we've had and continue to have together. You have all brought so much joy and laughter to my life, and I am thankful to be constantly surrounded by great people.

To Brian Wright, thank you for taking on this project and helping me share my story. I couldn't have written about my life in this way without you, and I'm blessed to have such a great new friend.

To the most beautiful and important person in my life – my wife Haley. You bring out the best in me, and none of this would be possible without you. Thank you for standing by me through thick and thin and for showing me how to be a better man. I love you more than words can describe.

And finally, thank you to my God and my Lord and Savior, Jesus Christ, for giving me a life I don't deserve. Your loving has carried me to the place I am today, and I pray that I honor you with my life's journey.

Made in United States
Orlando, FL
03 December 2021